The Tax Guardian

The Tax Guardian

Walter F. Picca

iUniverse, Inc.
Bloomington

The Tax Guardian

iUniverse books may be ordered through booksellers or by contacting:

iUniverse
1663 Liberty Drive
Bloomington, IN 47403
www.iuniverse.com
1-800-Authors (1-800-288-4677)

ISBN: 978-1-4620-1965-6 (sc)
ISBN: 978-1-4620-1966-3 (hc)
ISBN: 978-1-4620-1967-0 (e)

Library of Congress Control Number: 2011907716

Printed in the United States of America

iUniverse rev. date: 07/27/2011

CONTENTS

FOREWORD

Some of the original blog postings have been corrected, revised, and updated.

OBAMA'S CHALLENGE   Revised & Corrected

He said—to restore the economy, save or create more than 3.5 million jobs in two years, and cut the federal deficit in half in four years.

His remedy—the $787 billion Stimulus Package—to start!

The first major defect: it contains $505 billion in spending and no tax increases to fund the spending.

The second major defect: it contains $282 billion in tax cuts during a fiscal year, when there is a record-breaking deficit.

The biggest: the $400 tax credit per worker earning up to $75,000 and $800 for joint filers earning up to $150,000—for two years: costing $116 billion. Those earning more would get reduced amounts. Although, it is $100 less than his campaign promise made in December of 2007, times have changed. It was a bad idea then, it is worst now—because of the growing monster National Debt.

Right now—more tax cuts are not justified. The 2008 figures are not available, but in 2006, the bottom 50 percent of taxpayers—earning up to $32,000—paid only an average of 3.01 percent of AGI in taxes. That is very low. The top 26 to 50 percent—earning up to $64,702—paid 7.01 percent: that is too low. The top 11 to 25 percent—earning up to $118,904—paid 9.36 percent: that is much too low. The 2008 figures would not much change. They are far below the statutory rates: the reason: tax deductions and credits, and Obama has added more. That is irresponsible. Forecasters estimate, when you add the cost of the stimulus package and the banking bailout—the deficit for 2009 will climb to $1.6 trillion: triple the 2008 deficit.

Obama's plan not only validates the Bush 2001 and 2003 tax cuts on income, but, he will add to them. His tax credits will add 16 million to the already more than 47 million filers, who pay no federal income tax—and they will get the $400/800 tax refund. On ABC's This Week: Speaker of the House, Pelosi, defended the Obama tax cuts, saying: But, they do pay taxes, the "payroll taxes." Listen, I explained that once before, I will again. The Social Security payroll tax—does not pay to operate the federal government: it is a government managed pension plan that benefits workers, when they retire. The difference, when you spend revenues from the income tax, there is no government debt created, when you spend or divert the S.S. paid-in-surplus for other government expenses—you create a debt. The problem here, the government is diverting the S.S. paid-in-surplus for other purposes and not including the debt—in the budget deficit. That is misleading the taxpayers: Bush did that for eight years. I sent Pelosi—a letter—informing her of my website: www.thetaxguardian.com—she failed to read it.

The two year $400/$800 tax credit in the stimulus package is badly designed for a number of reasons:

1. The tax credit paid in weekly installments on wages up to $75,000 for singles and $150,000 for joint filers is not justified, when the projected budget deficit for 2009 is $1.6 trillion.
2. It places the extra cost and burden of making these weekly payroll changes on the employers for 2 years: for very little benefit. It is vexing to compute the tax credit—for employees who change their jobs, work part of the year, work for different employers, etc.
3. It is extra work and cost for the IRS to audit these millions of returns for mistakes or accuracy: the tax code must be rewritten, forms need to be changed, computers reprogrammed, etc
4. Taxpayers in the phase out zone: from $75,000 to $95,000 for singles and $150,000 to $190,000 for couples; certainly, do not need or deserve a tax credit in these times: the amounts small and

next to nothing—and at these levels would not stimulate much increased spending.

5. The $400 tax credit comes from a reduction in the income tax withheld by the employer: the problem: workers who pay no income tax get a tax refund. They get a check from the government, when they file their tax return. In this case, it is not a tax credit—as described—because, no income tax is paid. It is wrong to define contributions to Social Security—a tax that supports the government. They are contributions to workers' retirement benefits. It is the same as premiums paid to a union or employer pension fund. The refundable tax credit—is more correctly—a government handout for low-income workers. It is wrong to call it a tax credit—or a MWP tax credit—or payroll tax off-set credit for those that pay no income tax. Handing out taxpayer money to those that have not earned it—and those that don't need it—to simulate the economy is hardly rational.

Obama's numerous tax credits in this bill also violate the basic principle of government—the Head Tax, which means: everybody who benefits from the government --should pay some tax on earnings—over what is required for basic needs. His tax credits increases the number of people the government supports and decreases the number of people who support the government—or pay taxes. These are pernicious tax credits. He is no JFK. His message to the lower and middle class; should be, spend less on yourself—so, you can pay your fair share of taxes.

His $282 billion in tax cuts to stimulate the economy and create jobs—will increase the national debt—and will do little to create jobs. Jobs losses are the result of, mainly, other causes; such as: trade imbalance, burdening employers with medical and pension costs, failure to modify labor contracts prior to bankruptcy, globalization, exporting jobs, private and public over indebtedness, income inequality, the concentration of wealthy at the top, unjust taxation, wrong government policies, bad debts left behind when the housing bubble burst, the global economic downturn, etc. Cutting taxes more—on 95 percent of taxpayers—to improve the economy is not the right solution. The government will get back—less than it gave out.

Compare Obama's $400 and $800 tax credit with Bush's up to $300 single and up to $600 couples tax rebate in 2001. Both were (bad) vote getting schemes—that add to the federal deficit. They are a worst idea now, because there is a big deficit and we are in two costly wars, whereas, in 2001—there was a surplus and no wars. Obama is off tract.

The second biggest, irresponsible tax cut in the stimulus package: the $70 billion AMT—one year patch. Because of the monster estimated deficit for 2009, it would have been better to let the AMT exemption revert back to the 2000 levels: $33,750 for singles and $45,000 for couples. The reason given—for the one year patch: to prevent AMT from snagging millions of middle class taxpayers. That is a stretch. Nearly 70 percent of benefits of AMT relief in 2009 will go to the richest 10 percent, earning over $108,000. That is why it was inserted by the Senate—it includes members of congress. It increases the exemption to $46,700 for single filers and $70,950 for joint filers—before triggering the 26% tax on income. It is irresponsible—to give a tax cut to the top 25 percent—reaching as high as $433,800 for joint filers—before phasing out; when the projected deficit for 2009—will be triple the 2008 budget deficit.

I believe the AMT exemption should be placed at the 2005 level, considering they were pushed too high under Bush and the current projected federal deficit. Although, I favor my AMT, which is more fair and simple.

What is urgent: raising taxes on these most able to pay: this will add to government revenues and lower the deficit. People who still have their job are not experiencing a recession.

Individuals earning over $50,000 can afford to pay higher taxes. They have been under taxes for 28 years or since Reagan. There is a lot of money available—but, it is concentrated at the top. To delay a tax increase here—until the economy recovers is irresponsible. Obama is going ahead with the wrong tax cuts—and back peddling on the right tax increases: that will add to federal deficits.

Since, two wars are in progress: I believe enacting the war surtax— H.R. 3948—to pay for the Iraq and Afghanistan wars—until they are paid for is the right thing to do. I would tell Obama—not to listen to the Speaker of the House, Nancy Pelosi. She is part lunatic (on this subject). And Republican John Boehner is worst. He is anti-tax, mostly, on the rich for any reason.

I also recommend—repealing the repeal of the estate tax—in 2010. Otherwise, the US government will lose $15 billion it is owed in back taxes [based on the 2009 level].

Right now—the estate tax exemption should be lowered to $500,000/$1 million, except for family farms and businesses and graduating tax rates installed. That is absolutely a fair and needed tax. I believe a combination heavy estate and/or inheritance tax are needed to collect back taxes owed and lower the deficit. Once, the National Debt is reduced below 60% of GDP; then, these taxes can be lowered.

I also believe repealing the Bush tax cuts and the failure to raise them; mostly on the wealthy, after the Iraq war began—that got us into this financial crisis to a large degree—should be the first order of business. Then, set about reforming the grossly unfair US tax code. IRS statistics shows: 7,389 federal tax returns with $200,000 or more in AGI reported no federal income taxes in 2005, 66% of corporations pay no income tax, the number of tax filers that pay no federal income tax has sharply increased from 18.5 percent in 1985 to 32.4 percent in 2004 to about 47% in 2009. The reason: congress keeps adding more tax deductions and tax credits to the tax code. That is one big reason why we have a $10.7 trillion national debt that is rapidly growing.

Obama's stimulus package contains nothing to reduce the deficit—short term. It did not repeal the repeal of the estate tax for 2010—and strengthen it, which is essential. It contains no tax increases to fund the spending programs. It contains no tax increase on those that can easily afford it. It did nothing—to close the tax loopholes and tax heavens that are being manipulated—that Obama promised during his campaign—to pay for the tax credits. Basically, it is a giant tax cutting, tax credit adding, and spending bill that balloons the deficit. No doubt, some parts are good; but the cost will override the good. The total cost of the bill $1.1 trillion, when you add the interest: $348 billion.

Tax wise—the stimulus package is a lemon: badly designed.

The entrenched plutocracy continues to have a stranglehold on lawmakers and president Obama is their African-American slave—or he has become one of them. He knows the headwinds are strong against raising taxes on the wealthy. They are needed now—not two years from now: individuals with AGI over $200,000 can easily afford a tax increase—in 2009. They are not suffering from a recession.

The Democratic Party platform plank on tax policy states: "We must reform our tax code. It's thousands of pages long, a monstrosity that high-priced lobbyist have rigged with page after page of special interest loopholes and tax shelters." But, when in office, they don't reform it—they add more pages, tax cuts and credits.

THE WAR SURTAX

War and tax increases go together like nuts and bolts. The problem: we have too many nuts in congress. Nancy Pelosi, Speaker of the House, is a nut. The Constitution gave Congress the power to lay and collect taxes. It has neglected its duty—by authorizing the Iraq and Afghanistan wars and not paying for them; the consequence, the rapidly growing National Debt.

Congress levied excise taxes on distilled spirits, tobacco, refined sugar, carriages, etc.—to pay the debts of the Revolutionary War.

Congress imposed taxes to raise money for the War of 1812.

Congress passed the Revenue Act of 1861—to pay for the Civil War.

Congress passed the War Revenue Act of 1899—to pay for the Spanish-American War.

Congress passed the 1916, 1917, and 1918 War Revenue Act—to pay for World War I. These three acts: raised the bottom rate to 6 percent and the top rate to 77 percent on income.

Congress raised taxes during World War II: the bottom rate to 23 percent and the top rate to 94 percent.

Congress raised taxes again—during the Korean War: the top income tax rate: 91 percent over $400,000.

Congress enacted a surtax on income during the Vietnam War: the top rate, for the most part, 70 percent over $200,000.

There is one exception: George W. Bush cut taxes during the Afghanistan and Iraq wars. The 2003 tax cuts, mostly favoring the rich, reduced the top rate to 35% over $365,700, the capital gains and dividend tax to 15%, and raised the estate tax exemption. To make up the difference—he purloined the Social Security and Medicare paid-in-surplus. He misled the American people: claiming his tax cuts lowered the budget deficits. The truth is: the National Debt shot up every year.

In 2007—he requested an additional $190 billion more for the war in Iraq and Afghanistan.

Three top Democrats reacted with a war surtax: it was a 2.5, 5, 11, and 16 percent surtax of one's tax bill. It was called: "Share the Sacrifice Act of 2007," because it imposed the tax on individuals, estates, trusts, and corporations. It was a fair tax—and would raise $140 to $150 billion per year.

But, Bush wanted the money—not the tax to pay for it. Up to this point: the US was paying for these wars—by borrowing. Rep. James P. McGovern (D-Mass.) said, every morning countries like China and India buy up this debt—further weakening our economy and our security.

He says, my colleagues will argue we should cut spending. He says: "That is not real. Are we going to eliminate the entire departments of Labor, Education, Health, and Human Services. That's what it would take to fund one year of the Iraq war." To gather support:

Three top Democrats: Obey, Murtha, and McGovern sent a letter to Members of Congress—here is part:

"Some people are being asked to pay with their lives or faces or hands or their arms or their legs. If they are being asked to do that, it doesn't seem too much to ask the average taxpayer to pay $112 for the cost of the war so we don't have to shove it off on our kids."

However, top Republicans quickly opposed the bill—along with House Speaker, Nancy Pelosi. She was opposed to the war. Rep. John Boehner (R-Ohio) described the tax as "one of the most irresponsible proposals I've seen in a long, long time." He is a worst nut---rated by the CTJ—zero. He is a tax-blocker on the rich for any reason. I have a question for this freakin bastard; if, soldiers of the poor and middle class, can give their limbs and lives for the war—you voted for; then, shouldn't the rich, like yourself, have their taxes raised to pay for it?

Look, Pelosi's excuse is lame. The Congress voted to give Bush the power—to invade Iraq: not liking the outcome is not a reason—not to fund it. The reality is: the war is ongoing—either, you or your kids will pay for it. The toppling of Saddam left the country in chaos—restoring law and order was an American responsibility—so long, as the Iraqis are doing their part. They did not at first—but, their determination is growing.

What is at stake here is: Operation Iraqi Freedom. That is what the funds are for. That is an honorable mission.

Here is what Dana Morino—spokesman for the White House or Bush said: "There's no need to increase taxes, the president has shown how if we prioritize and if we get the spending bills done in a clean way, we can actually have a surplus in our budget by 2012."

You see how ridiculous: this statement is now—when, the budget deficit soared to $455 billion in 2008—not counting off-budget expenses—and the revised GDP shrank 6.2 percent in the fourth quarter and the recession is deepening.

Rep. David Obey (D-Wis.) said, "This is the first time in American history that when a president has taken a country to war and said 'by the way folks, we're going to have to sacrifice and the way to sacrifice is cutting taxes.' It makes no sense." That is exactly what I have been saying. Bush is an idiot. Here are presidents that enacted taxes to pay for wars:

Lincoln established the first graduating income taxes, taxes on inheritance, and corporate dividends to finance the Civil War.

McKinley raised taxes to pay for the Spanish-American War.

Wilson massively raised taxes for World War I.

Roosevelt raised taxes for World War II.

Truman raised taxes to pay for the Korean War.

Johnson enacted a Vietnam War surtax.

Tim Russet—said to President Bush—in an interview on *Meet the Press:* "Every president since the Civil War who has gone to war has raised taxes, not cut them." Bush responded: "it is not true"—and gave disingenuous examples, such as: there were no tax increases to pay for the Persian Gulf War. The reason: the US bore only $7 billion—or 12% of the cost: the rest was borne by Gulf States and coalition members. Compare that to the Iraq War—costing $624 billion so far.

Bush is only president that would not pay for the wars—he started— saving the tax cuts; mostly on the wealthy, was more important to him.

Since, Iraq and Afghanistan wars have not been paid for and are unfinished—it is a good time to pass the War Surtax.

Enacting the War Surtax—should have been—one of Obama's top priorities—or undoing the Bush tax cuts, primarily, on upper income Americans—this year. That would be—even—better plan. Lawrence Summers, Director of the National Economic Council, says: "The country cannot afford them long-term"—on *Meet the Press*. He equivocated on the timing. I agree with Rep. Pelosi: we must repeal them now—this calendar year. NBC's David Gregory said, Why not put the expiration date off unto 2013? He is on the side of the wealthy.

The following week on *Meet the Press:* Senator Kay Hutchinson described the cuts in the dividend and capital gains taxes—"good tax cuts." She is a Republican Texan plutocrat—Bush's soul mate on tax issues: rated 0% by the CTJ (worst score possible). Actually, they are the worst and most immoral of all tax cuts—made and extended during the Iraq War—highly favoring the top 5 percent—that includes the congress. She voted for them, their extension, and voted against the repeal to fund the military during the war and cut the deficit. That is despicable.

She voted Yes—to give Bush the power to invade Iraq. Like Bush—she doesn't like paying for it—and most Republicans.

Who gets the most benefit from National Defense—the rich. They have the most to lose. The top 1% owns more wealth than the bottom 90 percent. Who does the fighting—not the children of the rich. Of the 535 members of congress—only about 5 had children servicing in Iraq in 2005—8 in 2007.

The war in Iraq—has been going on longer than World War II—and we still haven't raised taxes to pay for it. It's time we start.

The Korean War cost $456 billion and the top income tax rate 91 percent during this period, the Vietnam War cost $518 billion and the top income tax rate 70 percent, for the most part: compare that to the Iraq

War costing $656 billion and growing: the top tax rate 35 percent; plus, dividends and capital gains were reduced to 15 percent: two of the biggest sources of income of the rich.

I would like to point out: from 1950 to 1980—through both wars—the national debt remained fairly constant. It was not until 1981—or Reagan: did the National Debt begin to grow every year—and spiked, dramatically, under George W. Bush.

Bush is lucky—he is not in jail: ordering a meal—and walking away without paying for it (i.e., the Iraq War). He gave himself, his cabinet, members of congress, executives, and rich political donors huge tax cuts—instead.

The direct and indirect cost of the Iraq and Afghanistan wars may run as high as $2.5 trillion—long term. The War Surtax is needed now—or the repeal of the Bush tax cuts—or both. Reducing the growing colossal National Debt should be a top priority—because the principle and interest payments are killing us.

How—we should end these wars is another issue.

OBAMA'S CHALLENGE #2   **Revised & Corrected**

Stop—wasteful spending!

Feb. 20th—President Obama addressed the nation's majors, saying: he would not hesitate to call them out—if, they wasted taxpayers' money and he would put a stop to it. On this, he said: I will not compromise or tolerate. And he said, every dollar of hard earned taxpayer money should be spent wisely.

    I think he should start with himself—by limiting his use of Air Force One—at taxpayers' expense. One reason I say that, Obama said: "Kennebunkport is on the south side of Chicago. We are going to try to come back here as often as possible....at least once every six weeks or couple of months."

    I hope he plans to fly VIP commercial and pay for these trips. Cutting government expenses—should begin at the top: I don't think the President—should get much more vacation time, than the average worker: 14 days. He can go back to the south side of Chicago—and see his buddies and play basketball when he is no longer in office. These trips are not official business.

    Obama and the Congress blasted Citigroup over a $50 million new jet—after receiving bailout money—and executives taking junkets at luxury resorts. But, what about the President. He is far worst.

    On Feb. 5th—he flew 114 miles to Williamsburg, Virginia on Air Force One to attend a retreat for House Democrats. He could have taken

Marine One at one-tenth the cost. This was a joy ride. It cost taxpayers more to fly him—than 200 members of congress on a chartered Amtrak.

Purpose of the trip: take a few photos, eat, drink, and talk.

The following week, he flew to Elkard, Indiana and back to the White House on Monday; to Ft. Myers, Florida and back to the White House on Tuesday; and to Peoria and Springfield, Illinois and back to the White House on Thursday—on Air Force One—to push his stimulus package: the cost: $100,219 per hour not including cargo planes, limos, helicopter, staff, armored SUVs for staff, security, etc.

UPDATE

The military, recently, pegged the cost to operate
Air Force One at $181,757 per hour.

On top of this: add the cost to fly to Andrews AFB and back to the White House on Marine One, usually accompanied by two helicopters. So, when you see the President wave—as he enters Air Force One—there is a lot more to this. These trips generally are accompanied by at least one C-17 cargo plane for his limos, the second for back up—in case of engine failure, and maybe a decoy, and may include a smaller jet for his aides and a second cargo plane for more vehicles. These trips required an advanced planning party. And, when the president lands: he needs a police escort.

I believe Press Conferences—originating from the White House is the proper place to make speeches to the nation. These four trips did not create one job—nor, did they change the mind of one Republican. Basically, they are ego-trips of the new president. He was greeted like a rock star—but, so were Hitler, Mugabe, and Castro when elected. But, is it justified?

One black woman at Ft. Myers: asked for Obama's help: she lost her house to foreclosure and was homeless. Obama walked up and kissed her. What good does that do? He should have handed her $10,000—out of his pocket—that is how much Obama wasted of taxpayer money in one hour. He lives in the White House with recreational facilities inside—at public expense. But, after 18 days in office, he is not satisfied; he flies his family on Marine One to Camp David in Maryland: for a one day vacation costing tens of thousands of dollars—during a recession and massive FY deficit. The cost to operate Marine One: $10,000/hr. It will be replaced with a VH-71 Kestrel costing: $400 million: 28 are on order. I heard on the TV news: these helicopters will be stationed at major cities across the United States—for the president's use, when he visits. This is an outrageous waste of taxpayer money.

UPDATE

The over $13 billion VH-71 Kestrel program cancelled.

On Feb. 13th—Obama flew his family on Air Force One to Chicago, his home town, for the weekend. This is the second family vacation after being in office—less than one month. This 2 day family vacation—will cost the taxpayers hundreds of thousands of dollars: the exact cost—confidential.

On Feb. 17th—Obama and his aides took two Air Force One 747s to Denver, Colorado—1,700 miles to sign the Stimulus Package: costing millions. On Feb 19th, he flew to Phoenix, Arizona, to make a speech; then to Ottawa, Canada. We are never told—how many other cargo planes and jets are used in these trips.

In February, Obama flew to 9 different cities—on Air Force One.

Obama said to the nation's majors: he would require accountability and transparency—in spending taxpayer money. What about himself: he should reveal what these trips cost—and how Americans have benefited.

For one thing, the signing of the stimulus package could have been done at the White House—saving millions.

I am not even sure—he did Americans a favor by pushing and signing the stimulus package. It has ill-advised tax cuts and credits. The cost goes on America's credit card.

Furthermore, does the president deserve two costly family vacations in the first month of office—during the worst financial crisis—since, the 1930s.

March 6th—Obama flew to Columbus, Ohio—to make a speech at the graduation of 25 police recruits—and bragged: the $1.25 million funds received from the stimulus package paid their salary for 1 year. Basically, he flew there—to pump up his image as America's Messiah. He failed to reveal: his trip on Air Force One may have doubled the cost.

Air Force One is the most expensive and ostentatious jumbo jet in the world and Obama loves to fly on it. He told House Democrats—at Williamsburg: "Thank you for giving me an excuse to use Air Force One."

This is no excuse—he wasted taxpayer money.

On the weekend: March 7th & 8th—he took his family on a second one day vacation to Camp David, a palatial presidential retreat in Maryland. Obama told free-spending Americans in his first press conference: "In fact, the party now is over." For him—it is just beginning. He is using presidential perks to the max. Marine One is not cheap either.

Maybe—it's time to bring back the guillotine—legally.

Bernie Madoff—should be the first one to go.

Obama is no different than Mugabe: throwing a lavish party for his birthday, when his nation health's system has collapsed, half the population is unemployed and hungry. Elected officials—sometimes change—when in office.

Poor boy—Obama—has become a big spender.

But, it not only the president—that is wasting hard earned taxpayers' money: it is also some members of congress. There are page after page of codels—i.e., congressional delegations that take overseas vacations—that are so called: work-related—at taxpayers' expense—and/or congressmen (or women)—that misuse and abuse the air force as their private airline. Then, there are those that use government issued credit cards—for personal use. The rats are everywhere: big and small.

It is time taxpayers say: No—more!

Posted 3/20/09

OBAMA'S SPEECH TO CONGRESS, FEB 24TH
Revised & Corrected

It was an outline of his economic and political agenda, lecture, or pep talk. By his smiling, waving, shaking hands, and signing autographs: he thought he was brilliant. However, I disagree with some things:

1. He said, "...I stand here tonight and say without exception and equivocation that the United States of America does not torture." He is wrong on this issue. Torture, sometimes—can be justified. Not, the kind of torture most people think of—used by tyrants and criminals—for evil reasons. But, harsh interrogation techniques to extract information from terrorists to prevent harm to a nation or people is a good reason. In this case, it is not torture: it is self inflicted pain or punishment—for refusing to talk. It should be a crime to refuse to talk or reveal information that would prevent a terrorist attack. To rule it out 100 percent is immoral, dangerous, and moronic. It must be kept as a threat—to make people talk, and used in certain circumstances—to counter terrorism that has the wrong agenda for the world: destroying property, injuring and killing innocent people, human rights abuse, etc.

Torture to prevent—the truth or justice—from happening—is the kind of torture that is wrong; not, if done to prevent the triumph of evil.

Three things make torture justified:

a. Their plans are secret.
b. Their designs are evil.

c. The person subject to interrogation has information—or most likely has—and refuses to reveal it—or co-operate with the investigation, after a discourse, explaining why such actions are wrong. I would play a video of Islamic clerics condemning such actions—I would give them an opportunity to speak with one. If, soft methods won't work—then go to hard.

It might not always work—but, it does sometimes. You should have no pity for someone—who would set off a car bomb in a crowded street—or cut off your head—if, you didn't convert—to his evil agenda.

Supposing you captured a top al-Qaeda leader—whose secret organization was plotting a chemical, nuclear, or biological attack on the West; Obama says, he would never torture a terrorist—to get that information. He is an idiot. He would rather protect terrorists—than, people from terrorism. Being a fluent and assertive speaker is one thing: being right—is more important.

Obama would fire a missile from a drone—to kill a terrorist—but, he would not torture one—to save innocent lives. He is a false moralist.

Torture must be kept as an option—the same as the death penalty and the atomic bomb—to prevent horrific crimes against humanity.

2. I don't agree with this statement, he said: "If your family earns less than $250,000 a year—a quarter of million dollars a year—you will not see your taxes increased a single dime. I repeat: Not a single dime."

The reason he said that—to be popular with 95 percent of people. He rather be popular—than tell the truth.

He cannot—keep his word—and do all he wants to do—without creating a growing meta-colossal National Debt.

His agenda is flawed: he wants to invest in energy, healthcare, and education: that benefits bottom 95 percent of taxpayers—without them paying a dime. That is wrong and irrational.

For the thousands of households with AGI up to $250,000—that pay little or no income tax: he is not going to change that.

He is not going to enact the War Surtax—even though, he has increased the defense budget, the Iraq War is still in progress, and he is sending more troops to Afghanistan. He will pass the cost on to his kids—like Bush.

He cannot reduce federal deficits—sufficiently—by raising taxes on the top 5 percent of taxpayers and cutting taxes on the bottom 95 percent.

The Bush tax cuts—on income, dividends, capital gains, and the estate tax—should be repealed this year. I also recommend: higher income tax brackets to 70 percent—as a means of reducing the growing gargantuan National Debt.

President Andrew Jackson, the founder of the Democratic Party—called the national debt—a "curse." Obama—sees it as a blessing.

Posted 3/24/09

OBAMA'S $3.6 TRILLION BUDGET
Revised & Corrected

First of all: it violates the principle of pay-as-you-go—he subscribed to in the Clinton debate. It spends far more than the government takes in. Here are his estimated budget deficits for 2009 and the next four years:

$1.75 trillion for 2009
$1.1 trillion for 2010
$912 billion for 2011
$581 billion for 2012
<u>$533 billion for 2013</u>
The five year total: $4.875 trillion

Obama thinks these budget deficits are necessary for economic recovery. I don't. They are too high.

One reason: the budget includes making permanent the so-called: "making work pay" tax credit of up to $400 for singles and $800 for joint filers. He calls it an offset—for payroll taxes—for low income workers—that he has extended to upper income individuals and families. I have said before and I will say it again: the FICA tax is not a tax that supports the federal government. It is a tax for the individual's retirement and Medicare benefits. I wish Obama would get it through his head. We, already, have the Earned Income Tax Credit—we do not need a second overlapping one. It is a badly designed tax credit: lower income families—rarely pay income taxes—and upper middle class families don't need a payroll offset tax credit.

He is no different than Bush: wanting to make his tax cuts, mostly on the rich, permanent. He wants to make them on the bottom 95 percent of taxpayers. The problem—that is an outdated campaign promise made in late 2007. Then, the estimated 2008 budget deficit was $250 billion.

The facts have changed—he has not.

If, the tax credit is made permanent: 50 percent of American households will pay no income tax. That is wrong. He cannot expect the top 50 percent of taxpayers to carry the bottom 50 percent. That is a bad tax code.

To bring these deficits down—to a manageable level—you need to reduce [wasteful] spending and increase taxes. That is a no-brainer.

He plans no tax increases on the wealthy for the year 2009 and 2010—even though, the budget deficits are over $1 trillion [est.].

He plans to wait to 2011—to raise the top two income tax rates to 36 and 39.6 percent. That is not going to do it. That is too little—too late. Individuals with AGI over $200,000 are not suffering from a recession. It is those who have lost their jobs—or unemployed.

This year is the right time to reverse the Bush tax cuts; particularly, on the top 5 percent of taxpayers.

People like Manny Ramirez, who will earn $25 million this year and $20 million in 2010 are not suffering from a recession.

And, they are not losing their limbs—like some soldiers—which are getting paid a hell of a lot less. Since, his estimated deficit this year is $1.75 trillion—four times the 2008 deficit—now, is the right time to raise the marginal income tax rates to 70 percent on income over $10 million. But, raising taxes on the top 5 percent is not enough. It hast to be on everybody—with some loose change.

He does not believe the bottom 50 percent of households—should pay one dime for national defense—even though, they benefit.

His tax proposals are flawed and skewed in favor of the bottom 95 percent: the opposite of Bush. Raising the income tax only on the top 5 percent—not until 2011—is not going to reduce budget deficits.

I think—some of his programs—like, healthcare reform—should be put on hold—until the deficits are lowered. One thing he can do—that does not cost taxpayer money: ban trans fat in processed foods.

Bush projected in July of 2008: the deficit for the 2009 budget would reach $490 billion. We are half-way through the fiscal year: the deficit already is more than $1 trillion. So, whether Obama is honest—or accurate—will be determined by how close his projected budget deficits—equal the total increase in the National Debt for each of the next five years. He says, his budget includes the full projected cost of the Iraq and Afghanistan wars: that is an improvement over Bush.

He is requesting $200 billion for the war in Iraq and Afghanistan: $75 billion in 2009 and $130 billion in 2010. But, there is no request for a war surtax—in the budget, even though the cost of the Iraq and Afghanistan wars are still unpaid and on the books—and he is sending more troops to Afghanistan. He will pass the costs on to his kids and grandkids. This is a tactical error.

He is like Bush—requesting money and no tax increases to pay for these wars. He would rather be popular—than honest. He prefers to duck the issue—spend now and pay later, when the economy gets better. I believe costs—will be harder to pay in the future—not easier: not only because, these huge FY deficits will accumulate and have a negative impact on the economy; i.e., the P & I payments; but, also because, the Baby Boomers are going to begin retiring in a few years and instead of a S.S. paid-in-surplus—taxpayers are going to have to repay the surpluses that were borrowed—to pay Social Security and Medicare benefits. Then, they are going to have a fit.

The present $2.5 trillion Social Security Debt that is on the books and growing is really the paid-in-surplus siphoned off to pay other government expenses and not included in budget deficits. That is deceitful—verging on fraud. Bush did that for eight years. However, I am not 100 percent certain, Obama will continue this practice and therefore, I would ask him this question:

How do you plan to spend the paid-in Social Security yearly surpluses?

UPDATE

Well, this is no longer a concern, because, Social Security had a $29 billion shortfall in 2010—and projected to run a deficit until the Trust Fund is depleted in 2037. Now, it is a question: how the federal government intends on paying for the $2.5 trillion, it borrowed from the S.S. Trust Fund—as the IOUs are cashed in to pay for annual deficits. Increasing the S.S. tax is not the right means: that is double taxation. It must come from non-Social Security taxation.

These are seven good tax proposals contained in his 2010 budget:

1. His proposal to reinstate the top income tax rates of 36% and 39.6% for taxpayers with high income in 2011.
2. His proposal to tax "carried interest", the manager's compensation for hedge and private equity funds investment profits—as income—rather than capital gains—is long over due.
3. His proposal to reinstate PEP—the phrase out of the personal tax exemption for taxpayers with high income in 2011.
4. His budget proposal to reinstate Pease—a reduction in the allowable deductions for taxpayers with high income in 2011.
5. His proposal to cap the value of itemized deductions at 28% for taxpayers with high income in 2011.
6. His proposal to raise the tax on capital gains and dividends to 20 percent—for individuals earning over $200,000 and couples over $250,000 in 2011—is semi-good.

I don't think long-term capital gains and dividends should be treated the same. The flat tax on dividends is a big tax break for big investors. It is fairer to put dividends under the income tax tables—where they belong. I don't believe—the double taxation argument is completely valid. Once, we determined—what the actual tax rate that corporations pay on profits—that pay dividends—then, perhaps, a percentage of dividends should be excluded from income taxation: to offset what corporations pay.

But, I believe—all six of these tax increases on high incomers should be enacted in 2009 to reduce the soaring National Debt. Delaying enactment 2 years, until 2011, is irresponsible.

I believe—the long-term capital gains tax rate should be raised to 25% over $100,000 and 35% over $500,000 to repay the government for the bailout and reduce the federal debt. The present: 85% percent for the self—and 15% for the government: doesn't seem fair to me.

7. His budget calls for making the estate tax of 45 percent—with the $3.5 million single and $7 million married exemption—permanent. That is better than total repeal—but not good enough. The exemption—should be lowered—and graduating rates applied: to collect back taxes owed from 1981. Here—Obama is off-target.

The budget calls for no change—in the gift tax (loophole).

In my opinion: the Obama budget blueprint is good and bad. He is acting boldly on spending—and cowardly on tax increases; the consequence, a giant growing national debt—for the next two years: that will do more harm—than good.

I believe taxes should be raised or lowered to balance the budget on a yearly bases—except for national emergencies and long-term investments for the good of the nation. Obama has ignored that principle—for the most part. However, congress has the power to make budget changes for better or worst.

UPDATE

Congress made it worst.

Posted 4/7/09

Surprise: I got a letter from Al Gore dated 1/13/09

He—i.e., his secretary answered my letter—posted on my blog: 12/8/08.

It, basically, says: he is too busy to answer.

Ross Perot, Peter G. Peterson, Warren Buffett, and Michael Bloomberg—did not answer by letter—sent in December of 2008—and posted on my blog: 12/8/08 and 12/29/08.

I was snubbed by all five—big shots!

Life Insurance—Loopholes   Revised & Corrected

Life insurance benefits, generally, are not taxed under the US tax code. Here are some examples:

1. The face-value of life insurance policies are not subject to the income tax without limits: $50,000, $1 million, or $10 million.
2. Proceeds from life-insurance are not subject to the inheritance tax—because, we don't have one [i.e., federal]: we have only an estate tax.
3. They are only subject to the 45% estate tax—if, the value of the estate including life insurance policies—exceeds the exemption: $3.5 million for singles and $7 million for joint filers [2009].

Six reasons for taxing life-insurance benefits:

1. It is a transfer of wealth—or income to the next generation—the same as a gift or inheritance.
2. It is used to by-pass the estate tax by setting up an irrevocable insurance trust. There is no justification for this loophole.
3. Income taxes pay the cost of government for one generation—not two; therefore, taxing life-insurance benefits is fair—because, it is a transfer of money, in the event of death—to the next generation.
4. It is not fair to tax income from wages and not income from life-insurance proceeds—not worked for.

5. It is not fair—to tax income from wages—to pay the cost of government—and not income from life insurance proceeds.
6. It is not fair—to tax income from wages—to payoff the National Debt—or unpaid taxes left behind by the deceased—and not income from life insurance proceeds.

Two fair ways to tax life insurance proceeds:

1. Subject lump sum life insurance proceeds to the Gift Tax: exclusion $50,000.
2. Life-insurance benefits paid in annual installments to individuals: subject to the Gift Tax.

Taxing life insurance proceeds to pay the cost of government and payoff the National Debt is fair—because, the insured owes part of it and the recipient owes part of it. The way the US tax code is structured right now: both these principles are abused and ignored. There is no income tax on life-insurance proceeds, no [federal] inheritance tax, the estate tax exemption exempts 99.7% of estates, and there are loopholes around the estate tax. And the consequence, the US government suffers a revenue loss—it is owed.

One exemption:

- Life insurance proceeds paid to tax-exempt institutions.

The US tax code is not fair. It cheats the government. There are too many tax credits, tax shelters, tax deductions, tax loopholes, tax free incomes, etc.—the result: the rapidly growing National Debt, as of 4/14/09, $11.17 trillion and has been growing an average of $3.84 billion a day since September 28, 2007. Higher taxes should have been enacted—back in 2003. The plutocratic regime of George W. Bush cut them instead. Now, we have to make up for those lost years.

UPDATE

The last I heard: he continues to insist: his tax cuts should be made permanent: he is America's Gaddafi: unyielding—no matter how wrong.

Posted 4/17/09

Road to Hell

Revised & Corrected

EU President Topolanek called Obama's stimulus plan: the "road to hell." He is right; if, he means: deeper and deeper into debt. The US Congressional Budget Office—seems to agree. It predicts Obama's budget will produce $9.3 trillion worth of red ink from 2010 to 2019. The reason: it is easier to spend money, than make money. That is a private/public foible. He is strong on spending and pusillanimous, when it comes to increasing taxes; probably—because, he is more worried about his ratings—and the Democratic controlled congress seems to agree. The House and Senate passed his $3.6 trillion budget, but did not enact all Obama's tax proposals [therein]. That is irresponsible, since, the projected deficit for 2010 will be well over $1 trillion. The danger—without tax increases to go with spending increases—debt will grow faster than GDP. That is the road to hell. He leaves all the Bush tax cuts in place until—2011. That might delight the people—now, but as yearly federal deficits accumulate—it is going to be hell to pay in the future. He predicts: economic growth—will out pace deficit spending—and produce more government revenues in the future.

He is willing to suffer $4.34 trillion in additional debt—in the next four years; i.e., including 2009—to cut the deficit down to $533 in 2013. The outdated 2009 Bush budget --should be modified this year. The off-the-chart estimated of $1.75 trillion deficit for 2009 --almost 4 times the 2008 deficit: makes it necessary to cut [wasteful] spending and increase taxes this year.

He has abandoned PAYGO—and is betting on the multiplier effect: that economic growth will out pace deficit spending—eventually—and produce a harvest of greater tax revenues. Basically, his plan: is to cut taxes on 95 percent and increase spending—to get out of debt. That is a flawed plan. He is ignoring the need for a war surtax. He is ignoring numerous sources of tax revenues. He is failing to consider: his projections of future economic growth—maybe inflated. There are copious reasons—why there are limitations on future economic growth, such as: the rapid depletion of our oil reserves, agricultural water shortages, foreign competition, etc. Letting debt soar—and betting: it will be easier to pay off in the future—is gambling against the odds. The potential for future economic growth is not as great as it was after World War II. He is ignoring the $98 trillion unfunded debt that is coming due.

He is appeasing—an angry electorate—rather than—being truthful. Being truthful—would make him unpopular. America has been on the road to hell—since, the 1980s—in terms of rapid growing National Debt: from 33% of GDP to over 70% in 2009—and Obama's 2010 budget will make it ultra-worst.

The truth is—the majority of Americans are overweight and spoilt. They want bountiful government services [and benefits]—and pay low taxes. They demand highest wages and buy goods made with lowest wages. They spend too much on themselves, which makes them think—their taxes are too high. Some eat so much—they have their fat surgically removed. They are pigs. Overweightness and over indebtedness are the same problem—lack of self-control.

I see a lot of people in line for free food—that are overweight and obese: that was not the case in the 1930s-40s [look at the newsreels]: the main reason: overeating. Obama said, everyone must sacrifice for the "greater good." That is opposite of his plan to cut taxes on 95 percent to win voters. That is the road to hell.

I would say: 60 to 70 percent of people should eat less—and pay more taxes: that would be a triple benefit: cut medical costs, increase government revenues, and better health.

Most Americans are not paying too much in taxes: they are paying too little. There are two tax principles:

1. The people should better manage their money—so, they can pay their share of taxes.
2. The government should better manage taxpayer money--to prevent budget deficits.

Obama believes—by cutting taxes and spending more, we will grow our way out of debt. He is betting double-down on red [deficit spending to win].

He is missing an opportunity to raise taxes on upper income earners in 2009 and 2010: they are not suffering from a recession.

Obama calls for funding the war in Iraq and Afghanistan—the contradiction: he does not call for a war surtax: that is the road to hell.

Obama is a confident, smiling, fluent speaking, people pleasing dimwit at times. Recently, he has made a couple of idiotic statements:

1. His aim: a nuke free world. He wants to fight wars with spears and swords. Nukes in the right hands—prevents bloody wars.
2. America is not and will never be at war with Islam.

There are over 150 different sects—which one is he referring to? Right now, we are at war with certain sects in Iraq and Afghanistan. I have never heard leaders of Islam in Arab countries—renounce Jihad, holy war, against the West—or advocate the freedom of choice in religious matters. In fact, certain sects are not only at war with the West and other religions, but with themselves for dominance.

UPDATE

After the New Year's bombing of a church in Egypt killing 21, Amin Germayed, the former Lebanese President, said: Extremist groups are waging "genocide" against Christians in the Middle East. Since 1972, there have been 3,098 killed by Muslims in America in 67 terror attacks. Thirteen attacks or attempts have taken place—related to Islamic extremists—since Obama took office—and numerous plots: proven and alleged. Of course, we are at war with

Islamic extremists, because they are at war with us: here and abroad. That is why we have a security check at the airport.

Obama believes the right path for America—is his bloody red-ink budget plan. That is the road to Hell.

He rather be dishonest—than, lose at the polls.

I believe—the war surtax and raising taxes, mostly on the rich, and cutting wasteful spending and getting rid of abuse and fraud—in 2009 and 2010—is the right path. The, nearly, four times bigger deficit for 2009; than 2008, demands drastic action now. Obama is taking a two year retreat—letting the deficit skyrocket.

This is proof: plutocrats continue to control the Senate—by the passage of an amendment to Obama's budget 51 to 48: that would increase the estate tax exemption to $5 million for individuals and $10 million for couples and lower the tax rate to 35%. That is shameful. Some legislators are willing to cheat the government to benefit a few—extremely rich. I believe—it should be lowered to $500,000 per person and graduating rates applied: to collect back taxes owed for the last 29 years.

But, this amendment—has yet to pass the House.

The House and the Senate passed Obama's budget for 2010, but, that does mean: congress will enact all his tax proposals—therein.

UPDATE

They did not!

HAVE WE GONE CRAZY—with tax-free income, income deferrals, deductions and tax credits?

This is an example—based on the 2009 tax code—of a married couple—named: Burock and Mechel with 2 children—filing jointly.

Burock, quite likely, acting on inside information: buys 21,000 shares of a $2 bio-stock and 467 days later, after the company received a $22 million deal from the US government—sells the stock at a 73% profit—or $30,660. Since, the couple were in the 15% income bracket: they will pay no long-term capital gains tax—or have zero tax liability.

Mechel, his wife, inherited $500,000 from her deceased father: that is tax free.

The couple invested $500,000 in municipal bonds at 6% for 6 months and earn: $15,000. That is tax free.

Total tax free income: $545,660

Their joint income from wages:	$75,000	. . . .$75,000
Above the line deductions:		
IRA contributions for 2:	$10,000	
HAS contributions for 2:	$ 2,000	
total	$12,000	. . . .$12,000
		AGI $63,000

Deductions (below the line):

Standard 2 x $5,700	=	$11,400
Personal exemption 2 x $3,650		$ 7,300
Dependent exemption 2 x $3,650		$ 7,300
Property tax deduction for non-itemizers		$ 1,000
total		$27,000. . . . .$27,000
	taxable income	$36,000

Tax on taxable income: $1,670 plus 15% over $16,700 = **$4,565**

Child tax credit: 2 x $1,000	=	$2,000
Child care credit	=	$1,200
MWP tax credit	=	$ 800
First time home buyers credit =		$8,000
Total		$12,000 minus tax credits $12,000

Tax Refund $ 7,435

They have total income of $620,660: a big part is tax-free, part is deferred, part is reduced by exemptions and deductions, and part is reduced by tax credits—and they without paying any federal income tax get a tax refund of $7,435. Tell me: Is that a wise (or fair) tax code—when we have an estimated $1.8 trillion deficit for 2009? Of course not, it is insanity. Lawmakers (or politicians) have undermined the tax code with tax-free income, tax deferred income, tax deductions and tax credits to appeal to voters—or get elected—and the US Government gets shortchanged: this couple with two children gets hundreds of benefits and services from the federal government: have a total income of $620,660 and pays no federal income tax—and gets a tax refund of $7,435. That is crazy.

Wait—there is more:

Obama has proposes a saver's tax credit of 50% up to $1,000—a person places in a retirement account.

A $4,000 college refundable credit

He wants to make the $800 MWP tax credit permanent

Expand EITC

Proposes 10% mortgage interest credit for non-itemizers

He wants to exempt tax on seniors up to $50,000, etc.

The lawmakers have destroyed the tax base that supports the US government—to get elected. If, Obama's tax proposals are enacted: more than 50% of filers will pay no income tax—and many will get refunds. Reagan and Bush destroyed the top of the federal income tax code with tax cuts mostly on the rich, Democrats and Obama—have destroyed the bottom with deductions and credits for the low and middle class singles and families.

The ecstasy-meth-pot-cocaine tax party must end!

Somebody has to pay the National Debt of $11.397 trillion—as of 6/10/09—and is increasing at the rate of $3.85 billion a day.

Posted 6/16/09

Demolition of the US Income Tax   Revised & Corrected

From 1861 to 1978: there were 28 revenue acts, after 1978, the mood of the country changed: there were tax relief acts—but, no more tax revenue acts. People became to loathe paying taxes—and wanted more tax cuts and benefits—i.e., for private and government employees—or civil servants. The consequence, the National Debt has increased every year, except one, since 1980.

Thomas Paine, the English, French, and American revolutionist and pamphleteer, said: "The greater one's income, the larger the percentage of it to be taxed." He is right.

The Revenue Act of 1917, signed by Woodrow Wilson, was close to the perfect graduating tax—or golden model. Harding and Coolidge, both Republican presidents, took the wrecking ball to the act: reducing the top marginal rate, in steps from 73% to 58% in 1921, to 46% in 1924, and to 25% in 1926. It was called the "roaring twenties". The stock market shot through the roof, most investors thought that stock prices "always went up". However, GDP and government revenues did not increase—significantly. The stock market crash of 1929—and the great depression that followed: proves lowering the top income tax rates—does not necessarily expand the economy and create jobs. GDP and federal revenues in 1920, under high taxation, were higher, than in 1931, under low taxation. The Revenue of Act of 1934—signed by Franklin D. Roosevelt—restored the graduating income tax to its original or near perfect form. It had 30 brackets: from

$0 to $1,000,000 and graduating rates: 4% to 63%. It served the US, with some modifications in rates and brackets through the depression, World War II, the Korean, and Vietnam wars—fairly well. The debt ratio to GDP was reduced from 120% in 1946 to 33% in 1980. Then, history repeated itself, Reagan and Bush, two Republican presidents, took the wrecking ball to the graduating income tax: removed and lowered the top marginal tax rates—and the debt to GDP has risen [back] to over 82%—and created a record breaking deficit for 2009—and a recession to boot.

And if, president Obama's budget plan for the next the 4 years is enacted: that percentage will continue to zoom towards 100%—into the red hot danger zone. It increases spending—cuts taxes on the middle class—and adds a number of refundable tax credits—adds a healthcare program for the 46 million uninsured, that is partially unfunded—and expects to lower deficits.

The debt-crisis is fourfold: the rich don't want to pay higher taxes, middle class want to pay lower taxes, lower income people—don't pay taxes—and most corporations: pay little or no taxes.

Here is what is going to happen; since, he is destroying the bottom base of the income tax with handouts and tax cuts and Republicans block taxes on the rich: congress will need to pass a Value Added Tax—to generate revenue: that is equivalent to a national sales tax.

One reason: Obama's proposals will create a new—majority of tax filers, that receive all the benefits of the government and pay no federal income tax and many of those—get a tax refund. That is not good. Whereas, the VAT is inescapable—i.e., unaffected by tax deductions and credits. The thing is: it is a regressive tax that hits low and moderate income people the most. But, a just tax—if, they pay no federal income tax.

That is what plutocrats want: they hate progressive taxation on income. They prefer the VAT: it does not hurt their pocket book—that much.

The lower and moderate income people—they want government benefits and pay little or no income tax: their leader Obama. He got most of their votes. He is similar to Mugabe, in some respects, catering to those that want something for nothing—or government services and handouts without paying a tax. [In some cases—it is justified—but].

Non-tax payers increased from about 18% in 1985 to about 40% in 2005 according to the Tax Foundation. Obama's tax proposals will push that number past 50%—reducing the number of tax payers to a minority.

That is the road to Hell.

Therefore, I am calling on taxpayers to wake up. The higher marginal income tax rates must be restored—and deductions and credits limited—or a fool-proof AMT passed—or lawmakers will be forced to stick taxpayers with the VAT, which acts as a national sales tax. It is hidden in everything you buy.

The problem: it is added to local and state sales taxes.

A progressive income tax is better and more fair; but, not if, tax shelters, tax deferrals, exclusions, tax deductions and credits—undermine it. The house of the US government will look like the leaning tower of Pisa, when the number of people that pay no tax—passes 50%. As it leans more and more—from less people paying taxes and getting refunds and gets heavier at the top—i.e., with public and foreign debt—the danger of the US government falling or going bankrupt—increases. It needs shoring up—that happens when taxes are increased, [wasteful] spending is cut, and tax revenues are sufficient to support the government (without deficits).

Recently, I read an article on Yahoo News, that CEOs were still taking private vacations on company jets—despite the financial crisis. What about the US president. It took three Gulfstream jets, three helicopters, and a motorcade, blocking traffic for hours, and over 600 secret service agents and police, so that, Obama and his wife could attend a Broadway play in Manhattan. Dinner and tickets: $96.50—paid by the Obamas. The estimated cost to taxpayers just for three jets: $23,000. The total cost—the White House will not reveal. He could have rented a DVD for a couple dollars and spent a nice evening in the White House. Spending up to $100,000 of taxpayer's money—for one night out on the town is extremely self-indulgent and irresponsible—given the state of the economy and the high federal debt.

Even more so, on Obama's recent trip to the middle east: his wife and kids hitched a ride on Air Force One—and they stop off—and take a 5 day vacation in Paris and London—and fly home at taxpayers expense: the estimated cost: $1 million.

I read on the Internet: "this WITCH is spending our TAX DOLLARS like everything is going GREAT!!!! 100 Secret Service, 20 SUVs, 4 jets and GOD knows what else...."

UPDATE

Obama flew to Afghanistan early in December, 2010, taking 14 hours, so the Obamas could spent their vacation in Hawaii at Xmas time: costing taxpayers $1,754,000 for 10 days.

This is clearly an abuse of taxpayer dollars, particularly at a time of high unemployment and soaring federal debt.

This is what he said to the nation's majors—Feb. 20th, 2009. He said, every dollar of taxpayer money should be spent wisely.....and he would not tolerate waste. It is an eight hour flight from Andrews Air Force Base—on Air Force One to Hawaii—costing $181,757 per hour: plus other costs. His wife, kids, and dog—took a second Air Force Plane, plus: a cargo plane for his limo, helicopter, SUVs for staff, etc.

The cost to taxpayer for Obama's four vacations—and Mechelle's five day vacation in Paris and London—for his first 2 years in office—will hit an all-time record.

The 28 hour round trip on Air Force One to Afghanistan to spend less than four hours with the troops Dec. 4th so, he could spend Xmas in Hawaii with his family and play golf and basketball: cost $5,089,196. That was a waste of taxpayer money. There was no military or political benefit.

The 18 hour round trip to Copenhagen on Air Force One cost taxpayers: $3,272,626: not including Marine One and two other air planes: no benefit was obtained.

These three trips cost $10,114,822—just for Air Force One.

On Feb, 20, 2009, Obama told the Nation's majors that he would call them out, if they wasted taxpayer money and put a stop to it. I wish—he would stop wasting taxpayer money. These trips were a waste and there are many more. Taxpayers should demand a Tally.

Here is what is wrong: the rich are getting richer and paying less tax, less and less people are paying taxes, more and more people are receiving handouts, (some) corporations are not paying their fair share—and the government is spending more and more—creating a staggering debt—that could result in US bankruptcy in 10 to 20 years.

It happened to GM—the number one world car maker. That was unthinkable in the sixties, seventies, and eighties.

It can happen to the US government—unless the right steps are taken to reverse de-taxation and increased spending. Obama is marching towards—more red ink—and increasing the number of people that pay no federal income tax—and get a tax refund. He is the co-begetter with Bush of the need for the VAT. It was unthinkable until Obama became president.

Even, his own adviser, Paul Volcher, supports it. He was the former Secretary of the Treasury for President Reagan.

I agree with Sen. Kent Conard (D-N.D.)—both the VAT and the high-end income tax increases should be on the table. But, I would go to the most able to pay first; then, to the less able.

The CBO estimates the National Debt will rise to $17.27 trillion—by 2019—under the proposed Obama budget. He favors four more refundable tax credits: MWP, tuition, mortgage interest, savers, and he wants to expand the child care credit and EITC, his health care plan is based on tax credits, and he wants to eliminate income taxes on seniors making less than $50,000. Obama would create a new diverse class of freeloaders. And the most insane thing: he wants to do this, when the nation is suffering an estimated budget deficit of $1.75 trillion. He is stealing from Uncle Sam—to buy votes.

He got 95% of the black vote, 63% Hispanic, 66% of under 30, and 68% of first time voters: that tells it all: these people want refundable tax credits and [free] government healthcare benefits.

Maybe—congress is not that foolish. Maybe, Obama is making promises—to win votes—he knows congress will reject. Maybe, Obama will see the Light—and change his mind. He recently said at Georgetown University: "We must build our house on rock not sand." Rock is operating the government on tax revenues: sand is operating the government on credit—or deficit spending. That increases the likelihood of collapse. Americans need to change their anti-tax attitude.

Posted 7/2/09

The Killing of the Estate Tax and the Partial Resurrection

Revised & Corrected

America has had a progressive estate tax since 1916, when President Woodrow Wilson signed it into law. It is America's form of an inheritance tax—called by opponents: the "Death Tax."

It goes back to the time of the Roman Empire: Cesar Augustus, the first Emperor from 27 BC to AD 14, instituted an inheritance tax. In 1795, Thomas Paine proposed an inheritance tax for England. He blamed the monarchy and the aristocracy for wealth inequality, social injustice, and the poverty of the mass of people. He had to flee to avoid arrest. Irwin Stelzer, an English-American economist, said: "The inheritance tax is one levy that makes good economic sense." Today, most industrialized nations of the world have one form or another: the UK, Germany, France, Italy, Spain, Greece, Korea, Poland, Japan, etc. The different between the estate tax and the inheritance tax: the estate tax is levied on the estate of the decedent—before it is distributed to recipients: the inheritance tax is levied on recipients after the estate of the decedent is distributed.

President Jefferson, Lincoln, Cleveland, Theodore Roosevelt, Taft, Woodrow Wilson, Herbert Hoover, Franklin Roosevelt, etc, either endorsed or used it to raise revenue.

The Stamp Act of 1797—was a transfer of assets death tax. It was used to pay off debts incurred during the undeclared war with France.

The Revenue Act of 1862—included an inheritance tax—to fund the Civil War.

The War Revenue Act of 1898—contained the Federal Legacy Tax to fund the Spanish-American War.

The Revenue Act of 1916 and 1917 included a 2% to 25% progressive estate tax to help fund World War I.

The Revenue Act of 1940—increased the estate tax to help fund World War II.

Besides, being a fair tax to redistribute wealth, where it is highly concentrated—it is also fair tax used to raise revenues, it is, particularly, a fair tax; if, a government debt was incurred during the life of the decedent; then, the estate tax is justified to collect back taxes owned—from the decedent's estate—before it is transferred to heirs.

This principle is lacking in the US tax code—it recognizes private debt—not public debt. If, the decedent was under taxed, the government has a right to make a claim on the estate—the same as private creditors. For the last 29 years, high income Americans have been under taxed. Since, the Reagan and Bush tax cuts the National Debt has soared every year, except one.

Look at it this way: the income tax and the corporation profit tax are the two main legs of a tax stool—that supports the federal government, when these two taxes fail to generate enough revenue—to pay federal expenses; then, the estate (or death) tax—acts as a third leg—to collect taxes owed from the estate of the deceased before it is transferred to recipients. The debt accumulated during life-time of the deceased: means the person was under taxed. What has happened: the third leg has been shortened—more and more --by Reagan and Bush—and no longer adequately supports the federal government—and back taxes owned by the deceased goes uncollected.

It is also fair to tax inheritances—to pay the current cost of government; since, it is a form of income. Why would you tax income from labor—and not inherited income. That does not make sense. The taxes paid by the decedent—does not pay for the cost of government for the next generation. I have stated this principle over and over again—yet, there are rich people—that want it repealed.

It is universally—recognized as a fair tax—to raise revenues for the government; but, it has unique characteristics—that other taxes lack. It acts to collect back taxes owed by the deceased—due to under taxation—and redistributes wealth that becomes concentrated in the hands of a few—and reduces the dangers of inherited wealth and power—or the transformation of a democracy into a plutocracy, a nation ruled by the super rich. That happened during the George W. Bush-era.

Wealth concentrated in the hands of a few is not a fair or good political, socioeconomic system. That happens; mainly, when the tax laws—favor the rich. The super wealthy in American have conducted a malicious campaign to repeal the tax. It is a goal of the Republican Party.

Since Carter, plutocratic lawmakers have dismantled the estate tax five ways (i.e., to the detriment of the nation):

1. Decreased the top tax rates.
2. Increased the exemption
3. Increased the annual gift tax exemption—that allows more wealth to be transferred during life—to avoid the estate tax at death.
4. Increased the life-time gift exemption
5. Increased the GST exemption.

Reagan and Bush—did all these things: plus—Bush tried repeatedly to repeal it permanently. Bush did repeal it for the year: 2010.

The Great Depression was not caused by high taxes: during the twenties, they were the lowest in eighty years. By 1929, the richest 1% owned 40% of the nation's wealth. In 1932, Herbert Hoover proposed raising the estate tax from 25% to 45% to help the unemployed and balance the budget: congress agreed.

The American people, he said: "know from bitter experience that the course of unbalanced budgets is the road to ruin."

From 1929 to 1933: GNP fell 31%: 7 million lost their jobs: about $2 billion in bank deposits were lost. Only 2 percent of Americans owned stock. The unemployment rate rose to 24.9%.

The newly elected—President F.D. Roosevelt raised the top estate tax rate from 45% to 60% in 1934 and to 70% in 1935—during the depression to fund various programs: CCC, TVA, NIRA, PWA, etc. and prevent family empires form taking control of the nation.

The Revenue Act of 1935—was called: "Soak the rich" tax. It was high compared to the past; but, wealth was concentrated at the top: 28 percent of the income went to the top 2 percent: only, 24 percent to the bottom 60 percent. More than half of all Americans lived below the poverty line. Therefore, redistribution was justified: to help the poor and create jobs. People, today, probably don't know this, but, a group of millionaires and businesses planned to overthrow Roosevelt and install a fascist government. That plan failed, when word got to the president.

The New Deal reduced the unemployment rate to 14.3% by 1937: the GNP grew 7.7% in 1934, 8.1% in 1935, 14.1% in 1936, and 5% in 1937. 1938 was a bad year, but it picked up in 1939. During these years of high taxes: the debt to GNP stayed about 40 percent—until World War II, when it shot up.

The estate tax was raised to 77% in 1941 to help fund World War II. From 1941 thru 1976, the top rate was 77 percent and the exemption: $60,000

During the Ford presidency, 1976 tax reform act—lowered the top rate to 70 percent and increased the exemption to $120,000.

The Economic Recovery Act of 1981—under Reagan—increased the exemption from $175,625 in steps to $600,000 in 1987 and dropped the top rate from 70 percent to 50 percent over a 3 year period.

Prior to 1976: the estate tax was paid by 7.65 percent of estates—after the 1986 tax reform act; roughly, 1-2 percent. That is a big drop!

The 2001 tax act, under Bush, lowered the top rate from 55% to 45% and increased the exemption in steps: from $675,000 to $3.5 million for singles and $7 million for married couples in 2009. For 2010—Bush repealed the tax for one year.

That was undone—in the Obama 2010 budget passed by congress. No Republican voted for it. It made permanent one tax rate of 45% with a $3.5/7 million exemption—allowing all, but 1/3 of 1% of estates to escape taxation.

UPDATE

*The underline part is a mistake. I explain this later in my posting: 7/29/10—**My Mistake.***

That is a decrepit, puny—or badly designed estate tax.

I believe the estate tax—considering the new estimated deficit of $1.85 trillion for 2009—and $1.3 trillion for 2010—should be fully restored.

I mean a progressive tax: from 10% to 65% with an exemption of $500,000/$1 million exemption for qualified family farms and businesses up to $3/6 million—operated by family members, and subject to the estate tax when sold or liquidated. And I would add second provisions (see My Mistake).

My second choice: replace the estate tax with a progressive inheritance tax with marginal tax rates from 10% to 65%, exemption $100,000

According to a 2000 economic study: 36.4% of estates worth over $1 million were untaxed capital gains. Based on the present tax code—i.e., the "stepped-up basis" of evaluating the estate's assets—that is never paid by the decedent or heirs. So, the estate [or inheritance] tax, fully restored is justified—to raise revenues.

Once, the National Debt is reduced to below—40 percent of GDP; then, adjustments in rates, brackets, and the exemption could be made.

The present rapidly growing $11.4 trillion National Debt is a product of gutting the income tax, corporation tax breaks—and shortening of the third leg of the tax stool (i.e., by estate tax exemption increases) that support the Federal Government.

The interest on the National Debt to June, 2009: $214 billion. That could be used to fund a national healthcare program.

Taxpayers get nothing—for interest they pay on debt.

The 2010 Obama budget—only partly—fixes the problem. The three legged stool that supports the government—has two weak legs—and an abnormally, short third and the rapidly growing US debt—that is adding too much weight on the stool.

President Obama sits on that stool—and is spending our tax dollars— like somebody on crack—singing: Don't Worry—Be Happy!

Now—is the time for fiscal responsibility!

People must realize, if the estate tax is repealed—paying off the National Debt must come from taxes on wages, income, and business profits of the living, rather than the dead who created most of it. The Reagan and Bush tax cuts, mostly, on the rich—and kept in place during two wars: created our growing Behemoth National Debt.

Therefore, a progressive estate [death] tax, mostly, on the rich, is a fair tax to collect—back unpaid taxes for 29 years.

Humpty Dumpty is Obama

He sat on a wall and had great fall—caused by his idiotic statements. The wall represents a solid foundation [truth, facts, or laws].

This is one of four: 5, 6, 7, etc.

He said on his 100th day in-office speech: that be believes: "Torture is wrong." Yes, some kinds—but not all.

Harsh interrogation techniques—which he calls torture—to obtain information to prevent secret attacks on innocent men, woman, and children—by misinformed Islamic militants, etc....

That is not wrong.

I don't agree with all the methods used at Gitmo—but, I would not ban water boarding—if it works—and used in selected cases. It is no worst—than, a taser gun used by police. It gives the sensation of drowning—but, seldom kills—or leave permanent physical damage. Obama believes it should be banned. He is forgetting those that are killed, burnt, and disfigured in terrorist attacks.

The thing is—terrorist can avoid torture or enhanced interrogation techniques by cooperating. They have a choice.

Victims of a car bomb—don't have a choice.

I would consult with other countries—that use torture—to get information: to find out what works—best. The purpose—not to obtain a confession by coercion—but to get information to combat terrorism.

But, I would try other methods first—before torture.

You cannot rule it out 100%.

Obama believes: it violates the articles of the Geneva Conventions. That is false. When, it was written in 1929—and last revised in 1949—terrorist that fly planes loaded with passengers into high rise buildings—did not exist in their imagination. This is a new breed of enemy combatants.

These articles refer to four types: prisoners of wars, seaman, civilians, and the wounded and sick—not terrorists .

Obama quotes Churchill, when London was being bombed to smithereens and had 200 or so detainees, he said: "We don't torture." World War II was a conventional war: England—knew the intentions of Hitler. These detainees—mostly likely, did not have high value secret information. Besides, England had a secret weapon, radar—that gave advance warning of German air attacks.

The war on terrorism is a different kettle of fish.

However, the British Secret Intelligence did use enhanced interrogation techniques during World War II. If, you could prevent a deadly attack—by the use of torture—it, would be justified—even, if it violated international law. If, that violates international law—than, the law is wrong.

International law—did not prevent the imperial troops of Japan and officers of the Gestapo of Nazi Germany—from torturing or mistreating prisoners and civilians. And, if we don't use harsh interrogations techniques: al-Qaeda or Islamic extremists, will continue to attack the West. They are brainwashed idiots that will not stop at nothing—but, eradication by force or enlightenment.

Opponents of torture say: it violates the UN convention against torture, adopted by the General Assembly in 1984—before the attack on the World Trade Center, the rash of airplane hijackings, bombings, and 9/11.

For that reason: it is not up-to-date—or obsolete!

Article 1—I believe, is intended to mean; because, it uses the words information and confession interchangeably, although not absolutely clear: prohibits torture for purpose of obtaining information or confession—to charge, convict, and punish; punishing someone for an act one has committed [having that knowledge], or suspected of having committed, or for any reason based on discrimination, such as: racial, ethnic, or religious.

It is a pre-terrorist-era document. It did not specifically prohibit torture to get information: for the purpose—of preventing a terrorist attack, or to bring other perpetrators of a terrorist attacks to justice. The reason: hijacking a plane full of passengers—to be used as missile—to bring down a building—had not been conceived—or blowing up a commercial airplane in flight—or blowing up a bus, or train full of commuters. These acts changed the world. Nations have a right to defend themselves by any reasonable means—including torture. I don't believe the United States --or any nation that has been a victim of a terrorist attack would sign or ratify this UN document—today.

Because, Article 2 states: there is "no exceptional circumstances, whatever" for the use of torture. That is equivalent to saying: you cannot defend yourself by using torture—or harsh interrogations techniques. The document is one sided—however, torture is a two-edged sword: there is evil and good.

Evil torture or cruel, inhuman treatment or punishment is used by tyrants against people—or dissidents seeking to gain human rights and fundamental freedoms.

Good torture or enhanced interrogation techniques is used by authorities to get information to combat terror groups—seeking or attempting to destroy human rights and fundament freedoms.

But, the no-exception rule or phase—relates back to Article I: for the purposes stated, which does not include torture—to get information to prevent terrorist attacks.

Because, of the possibility of secret-mad organizations getting their hands on nuclear, biological, and chemical weapons—exceptions need to be made—to protect a nation against these attacks.

I am not approving torture—for revenge, punishment, repression, discrimination, or to get a false confession. These are evil. I am approving the used of torture or enhanced interrogation techniques—to prevent terrorist acts and bring perpetrators to justice. If, it is not severely painful or life threatening: it probably won't work. The good thing, it can be avoided—by cooperating. It is no different than the death penalty or the use of the atomic bomb—when, justified to save lives.

Evil torture and good torture are like murder and the death penalty: one is a crime; the other is legal. There is a place for enhanced interrogation techniques—or torture—as some would call it: the same as the death penalty and the use of the atomic bomb.

If, the UN document says: you cannot torture—i.e., use harsh interrogation techniques—to get information to protect your nation from acts of terror, but you can kill the enemy using guns and bombs. It is a flawed document.

Article 2's—no exception rule—is analogous to saying: killing is never justified—even in war: the problem with that: you cannot defend yourself—from an evil person who will kill you. That is absurd.

Because, the world is becoming more dangerous—i.e., with the great harm—that small devices, or vials of chemical or biological weapons can cause in the hands of radical-hate groups—there needs to be exceptions.

Obama believes: it is alright to kill terrorists—it is not alright to used torture or enhanced interrogations techniques to save lives.

Obama would not torture one terrorist—to save the lives of 100 people—or 1,000; because, he says: it not consistent with our values. He is wrong.

When asked by Mark Knoller, a CBS reporter: "And if part of the United States were under imminent threat, could you envision yourself ever authorizing the use of those enhanced interrogation techniques?"

Obama backpedaled and said, "…when I made the decision to bar these practices, this was based on consultation with my entire national security team…." He is putting the blame on them. This is his baby.

There is no logical defense—for these idiotic statements. Torture—i.e., enhance interrogation techniques—did save lives during WWII.

I agree with President Sarkozy of France—Obama is inexperienced. Never served in the military—never been a victim of a terrorist attack. He is a few thousand genes short of being an American. Torture is right—only, if you are on the right side; obviously, Hitler, Mussolini, Hirohito, Mao-Zedong, Pol Pot, Ho Chi Minh, Idi Amin, Saddam Hussein, Omer al-Basher, King Jong Il, and others were [or are] not.

Based on his idiotic statements, he is not qualified to be the Commander-in-Chief. He is a rash, glib, over confident—Egg-Head—that has fallen off the wall and all the king's men can't put his broken egg-head back together again. His statement: torture is never justified: is indefensible, irrational, dangerous, and immoral. It can be justified in cases that meet the criteria, to save lives, to prevent an attack, to bring perpetrators to justice—to protect human rights and fundamental freedoms—the same as the death penalty—or use of the atomic bomb.

Posted 8/10/09

Obama's Tax Proposals/Changes—so far.
Revised & Corrected

The first two tax changes: the 2 year $400/$800 MWP tax credit—contained in the $787 billion stimulus package—and the over generous increase in the AMT exemption for 2009 affecting; mostly, the top 10 percent.

Both of these and are bad—and will add to red ink.

According to the Center for Budget and Policy Priorities: "Tax cuts do not come remotely close to paying for themselves."

Reagan and Bush proved that does not work. It might work temporary; but, the debt it creates—counteracts the temporary benefit in the future. The big debt created by the Reagan and Bush tax cuts are dragging down the economy—and limits what the government can do.

Then, why does the Obama Administration make them? Democrats do it—to get votes—or elected. Obama blames Bush for the huge deficit—he inherited; yet, his budget allows them to stay in place until 2011.

I believe—excessive taxation—might thwart economic growth; but, we don't have excessive taxation. We have under [federal] taxation.

Obama's worst tax proposal—to extend the Bush 2001 and 2003 tax cuts for individuals earning under $200,000 and households earning under $250,000—permanently. According to one estimate, that will add $3.2 trillion to the national debt over the next decade. This indecent proposal was made to get votes.

The Bush tax cuts were predicated on projected future surpluses.

The Obama tax cuts are predicated on future meta-mammoth deficits. This does not make sense.

His biggest mistake—putting off raising the top two tax brackets to 36% and 39.6% until 2011. I believe FDR would have raised the top bracket to 70% in 2009: to reduce the $1.75 trillion projected federal deficit. Obama is no FDR.

Obama blames the 2009 deficit on Bush, but at the same time leaves his tax cuts in place and adds to them: that is voter appeasement—not, doing what is best for the country—or the federal government.

All Bush tax cuts on income should be eliminated in 2009 and the tax code redesigned. They are based on overly, optimistic, economic forecasts made in 2001—that did not materialize. They are clearly more unjustified now. The revised projected total deficit for Obama's four year term of office: $4.58 trillion. The reason for these huge budget deficits: the government is spending too much—Americans are not paying enough taxes—about 60% of personal income escapes taxation. The reason: statutory income tax rates are not levied on net income or AGI—they are levied on income reduced to a fraction of net or total income by tax free income, itemized deductions, tax credits, exclusions, and deferrals.

Also, like individuals, there is a big gap in what corporations actual pay and the statutory rate. The 275 largest and most profitable corporations: paid an average of 17.2% in 2003—i.e., down from 21.4% in 2001 and down from 26.5% in 1988.

Facts demand a U-turn in 2009—Obama has made only a slight change in course—that is going to lead into a tar pit—of meta-colossal debt.

However, the congress had the good sense—not to make permanent the MWP tax credit—costing $600 billion over ten years and junk Obama's promise—to eliminate income taxes on seniors earning up to $50,000. That was pure nuts.

The congress failed to eliminate corporate tax havens—that were being manipulated—to pay for the middle class tax cuts – that Obama promised in his campaign. These tax cuts should be contingent on eliminating these corporate tax havens. These tax havens cost the US government an estimated $100 billion in tax revenues in 2008—according to a Senate report. I read: we might see action by December.

I read: Obama's proposed 28 percent cap on the value of itemized deductions for singles with AGI over $200,000 and married couples: $250,000—flew like a lead balloon in Congress. I agree—if, for the purpose of funding healthcare reform. What is also needed—is the repeal of the Bush phrase out of personal exemptions and the phrase out of limits on itemized deductions for high incomes—contained in EGTRRA (2001)—this year—or the adoption of a foolproof AMT. Here are some reasons:

The [revised] estimated deficit for 2009 and 2010: $3.1 trillion—one of the main reasons: US legislators have gutted the US tax Code.

The average income tax paid by the top 2 to 5 percent: 17.2% in 2007. That is far too low. The effective rate is close to the statutory rate on the second income bracket from the bottom.

In 2005, IRS statistics show 7,389 federal tax returns with $200,000 or more in AGI reported no federal income taxes. The big reason: lawmakers keep adding overly generous tax deductions.

The problem with the 28% cap: it makes the rich pay for healthcare for the 46 million uninsured that receive it—without them paying a dime in taxes. That is Obama's campaign pledge—that is unfair tax, in terms of its purpose. I believe higher progressive tax rates on all brackets—is a fairer tax. I don't believe in pinching the rich—for this and that. These costs can be handled by the graduating income tax.

But, in lieu of higher rates, the 28% cap on the value of itemized deductions is good—if, done to reduce budget deficits—and [best] enacted in 2009: better both—to reduce the deficit.

One thing, the overweight and obese can do—themselves—to cut [government] healthcare cost and improve one's health: go on the monkey diet (i.e., cut calories). That does not require much intelligence.

Obama's next mistake: not attempting to raise the capital gains and dividend tax to 20% for high incomes until 2011. That is irresponsible. Congress continues to give tax breaks to the rich and superrich—despite the record breaking federal deficit for 2009 and 2010.

To do this correctly, dividends should be placed under the income tax tables, where they belong. I would not consider making a reduction for corporate profit tax paid -- when the individual income top tax rate is 35%—half of what it should be. And, the long-term capital gains tax should be 25 percent over $100,000 and 35 percent over $500,000 --considering the $12.9 trillion the federal government has committed to economic recovery: 80 percent for the self—and 20 percent for the government— cheats the government. It should get back all of its investment.

Why, should income from labor be taxed progressively—and income from capital gains—flat. That is a tax break for the rich.

Good—that the House did not pass the outrageous hike in the estate tax exemption to $5 million for individuals: $10 million for joint filer and the lowering of the tax rate to 35% from 45%—passed by the Senate.

UPDATE

Unfortunately, it was passed by Congress in 2010.

So far, Obama's and the congress's tax cuts and spending have not led to higher tax revenues. Projected deficits have been revised upward: $1.8 trillion in 2009, $1.3 trillion in 2010, $929 billion in 2011, and $577 billion in 2012: totaling $4.606 trillion. They are irresponsible and will end in either: drastic cuts in outlays, higher taxes --or US bankruptcy in the future, if continued.

Debt is like obesity—the longer you let it go—the harder it is to correct. Obama is OK with letting the US government get heavier—more obese—with debt. He is not doing enough to reverse the trend now.

To him—it is more important to keep his outdated campaign promise: 95% of Americans—"will not see their taxes increased a single dime." He rebuked the Treasury Secretary, Tim Geithner, for suggesting such a thing on ABC's—*This Week*. That shows Obama is an idiot sometimes. I agree with National Economic Council Director, Larry Summers, he said on NBC's—*Meet the Press*: "it is never a good idea to absolutely rule things out, no matter what."

At the DNC in 2008—Obama pledged: to cut taxes for 95% on all working families. Then, the estimated deficit for 2009 was $487 billion—

it went up to $1.2 trillion in January 2009, and in his State of Union Address, he repeated: "not a single dime (more)" in taxes for 95 percent of Americans: the latest estimate: $1.85 trillion. The facts have changed: Obama has not.

He is more interested in his political career—than, what is good for the country: promising to cut tax cuts for the middle class—during a time of rising budget deficits—and providing healthcare for 46 million uninsured—without the bottom 95 percent paying a dime—is insane. He is just delaying the day of payment. The next president will face Bush's big debt and Obama's meta-giant Debt.

Troops will not leave Iraq until 2011 and the war in Afghanistan is not over and expanding: the cost of these wars is still on the books: it is time to raise taxes to pay for them. He thinks it is permissible to add $7.2 trillion to the National Debt from 2009 to 2019. The danger here: there could be another economic contraction in the next 10 years. The accumulation of that debt added to the present National Debt—is going to put a heavy strain on the economy: stunt, drag down—rather than spur. He believes his budget plan will generate more government revenues and cut the deficit two-thirds by 2014.

He is not factoring in the monumental federal debt—he is creating in the meantime: the ratio of federal debt to GDP will increase—and it is going to be a lot harder to bring that down in the future. It is an unhealthy expansion of the economy: debt will increase faster than GDP. It makes life easier now—and harder in the future: a mega-colossal debt repayment. I read on the Internet: "Last year, it took all the taxes paid by all the individuals West of the Mississippi River just to pay the interest on the National Debt...." The line will move more to the East—in the future.

President Obama can be compared to Governor Schwarzenegger: he demolished the car license tax increase—in 2003—an artifice to get elected: it created temporary tax relief. Look at California 6 years later: it has projected deficit of $14.4 billion for 2009-10. It is worst off.

President Obama, 10 year budget plan, is the promoter of the biggest government tax-cutting, big-spending, healthcare, debt-reducing fantasy—of all times.

He blames Bush—but, he is not stuck with the 2009 Bush budget: he can amend it: he has only made minor changes—big changes are needed: meaning: dumping the Bush tax cuts—now—and reform the entire tax code.

Posted 8/26/09

THE SODA TAX

A tax on sodas and sugary fruit drinks to prevent obesity and related diseases is a good idea. I believe mankind would be better off—health wise, if all refined sugar and carbohydrates were banned from the planet. But, that is not likely to happen. I read on the Internet: it is a Myth: "Eating too much sugar causes diabetes"—the website: the American Diabetes Association. That is false. The medical profession has been reluctant to admit the link between sugar and diabetes. They are in the business of treatment—not prevention. The ADA claims, "However, being overweight does increase your risk for developing type 2 diabetes." That is true—in part. Obesity is caused by overeating—any food. But, there is something pernicious about sucrose and high fructose corn syrup added to sodas. It is a major cause of diabetes—as well as obesity.

For that reason: sodas should be the first food to be taxed; since, it is not only a cause of obesity; but, more directly—diabetes. In the last ten years: the rate of new cases has doubled in the United States: more than 23 million are diabetic: 57 million are pre-diabetic—a huge potential medical cost.

For example, cheeseburgers could be a cause of obesity and the clogging of arteries—but, not necessarily diabetes. Since, it is not a high glycemic food. Sugar is the culprit—in sodas—or sweetened beverages. It is also a cause of obesity; since, the body turns excessive carbohydrates into fat. That is the main distinction.

There is a proliferation of sodas and sugary drinks in the market place, such as: a new vending machine with 100 different favors, Gatorade, Red Bull, ready-to-drink teas, sugar laden fruit juices—and the latest type: vitamin water with 13 grams of sugar per 8 oz serving. Sodas and sugar added fruit juices are marketed—almost everywhere: in supermarkets, pharmacies, gas stations, discount stores, restaurants, etc. Most markets place a refrigerated display case near the check out.

Consumption is on the rise in America. Data from the US Department of Agriculture shows the average per capita consumption of carbonated drinks rose more than 450 percent from 10.8 gals. in 1946 to 49.2 gals. in 2000. The typical person now consumes 190 calories a day from sugary drinks—some none—some multiple soft drinks. There is the danger. The U.S. ranks first among the countries of the world—in consumption of sodas.

Supermarkets offer an assortment of sizes: 8 oz, 12 oz, 16 oz, and 20 oz bottles, in pacts of 6 or 8—and 12 packs of 12 oz cans of different flavors and brands. There are 1, 2, and 3 liter and 1 gallon bottles—prominently, placed in different isles throughout the stores. Once purchased and taken home and put in the refrigerator: it is easy to take out a cold drink. Beside home consumption: fast food restaurants offer small 16 oz, medium 20 oz, and large 32 oz sizes—with free refills, and combination meals with a soda. Sodas taste good and give a quick boost of energy. It is an American habit—or craze. Herein lies the problem: the health dangers—of high glycemic drinks are not immediately recognized. Drinkers reason; if, it taste good and gives you energy: how can it be unhealthy. The problem: the ill-effects takes years to manifest.

The pancreas reacts—to sugar intake—by pumping insulin in the blood stream—and too much insulin—too often—has health consequences: not seen all at once—but, 10, 20, 30 years down the line. One of those long-term consequences: the overworked pancreas—stops producing insulin or the body becomes resistant to insulin. The body uses insulin to help convert sugar into energy. When, it fails to do its job: that condition is called: diabetes. The frequent elevation of blood sugar levels—caused by drinking sodas—results in insulin resistance—and/or pancreatic burnout. Therefore, a tax to reduce consumption is good.

In the 1950s—a bottle of soda was 6 and 1/2 ounces and went to 8 oz, 12 oz, 16 oz, and 20 ounce sizes: then to the 32 oz Big Gulp—then, the 44 oz Super Gulp—then, the 64 oz Double Gulp. It is cheap (i.e., compared to nutritional drinks), taste good and gives a quick energy burst. But, it has hidden health risks.

Yet, the beverage industry—hates the soda tax—they fear it would reduce sales (or profits). They come up with clever arguments, like: "Taxes are not going to teach our children to have a healthy lifestyle." It might, if taxes were used to pay for educational programs in schools—warning of the risks of sucrose, high fructose corn syrup, and other artificial sweeteners—used in sodas.

Health gurus—for many decades: have warned of the dangers of excessive consumption of sugar and science—now agrees: there is a link to a number of human health problems—including obesity, syndrome X, diabetes, cancer, blindness, hypertension, kidney failure, cardiovascular diseases, amputations, etc. And, today many nutritionists and MDs—say: it should be avoided—or eliminated from the diet.

Michael Jacobson, executive director of the Center for Science in the Public Interest, said: "Soda is clearly one of the most harmful products in the food supply, and it's something the government should discourage the consumption of." A regular 12 oz can of Coke contains 140 calories, 39 grams of sugar, in the form of high fructose corn syrup. Read the label.

The typical person now consumes 190 calories a day from sugary drinks—according the NY Times: based on C.D.C. data. Let's do the math: 190 calories times 365 days equals 69,350 calories a year: one pound of fat equals 3,500 calories: that is about 20 pounds of fat a year—unless burnt off. That explains—in part: why seventy-three percent of Americans are overweight and obese—they don't burn it off. In fact, the US has the highest obesity rate of any country in the world: 30.6 percent.

Researchers, led by Sara N. Beich, conclude: the increase in the consumption of sugar-sweetened beverages in the US—parallels the rising prevalence of obesity and type 2 diabetes. I might add: medical cost are also rising in the US and has the highest per capita of any nation in the world.

I read on the Internet, people say: the tax is an infringement on personal liberty, unfair, regressive because low-income people drink it, imperialism, etc. It might be unfair, if one pays for his health or medical care. It becomes a fair tax—when it is paid for—or subsidized by others.

In 2007, the estimated cost of treating diabetes: $178 billion: sodas are a major cause. Sodas have a higher glycemic index that most solid foods—and are devoid of nutrients; so, a tax on sodas is a good idea.

The purpose of the tax: threefold.

1. reduce consumption
2. pay the increase cost of medical care on those—that drink sodas and /or sugary fruit drinks
3. reduce public medical cost

I believe: a 1 cent tax per ounce is a fair tax: to accomplish these three objectives.

Why—it is not likely to pass—right now—leaders of the beverage industry are asking members of congress to defeat it, the public is not fully aware of the health risks, and lovers of sodas and sugary-energy drinks will cry foul. I have seen kids—throw a temper tantrum in restaurants—if, their parents deny them—a soda. But, the problem—they give in.

That happened in New York: Governor David Peterson dropped his proposal for an 18% tax on sodas—because of an outcry from the beverage industry and New Yorkers. He is a weak and blind governor.

Even, ex-president Bill Clinton has come out against the tax: his main goal: public popularity. He says: it is not the way. He may be suffering from reduced mental capacity. There is a picture of him—on the Internet—shaking hands with the CEO of Coca-Cola. If, he knew anything about health and nutrition: he would not have needed quadruple heart-bypass surgery. His Alliance for a Healthier Generation has made a deal with the beverage industry to remove sodas from school vending machines. That is a step in the right direction. But, it is not going to reduce total consumption—much. The drawback—it does not include diet-sodas.

Ralph G. Walton, M.D. says: "It would be especially tragic if an attempt to improve the health of our children led even greater exposure to this highly toxic product." He is referring to aspartame—used to sweeten diet sodas. It is a neurotoxin. Dr. Janet S. Hull's website: list 92 different side effects associated with aspartame. It has no business being sold in school vending machines.

Clinton told ABC News, "I'm doing everything I can on this obesity thing." No, he hasn't. He has not shaken hands with Michael Jacobson, Executive Director of the Center for Science in the Public Interest, who is advocating a tax on sodas.

Clinton said, "I think the better thing to do is to give incentives right across the board for prevention and wellness."

That is part of the solution, but.....

People will like him—because of ignorance—or willful violation of dietary laws—I continue to drink sodas; habitually, until—the damage it does—shows up years down the road. By the way, who paid for Bill Clinton's quadruple heart by-pass surgery and following up surgery called: decortications, stints, etc.—and how much did it cost?

That times every citizen is unaffordable.

UPDATE

I would add Zsa Zsa Gabor to the list: stoke, hip replacement, leg amputation, frequent hospital admissions, etc. All or much of this can be prevented by education—and right to die counseling.

Is there something wrong with these figures?

House Mortgage: $25,000 per month

Medicare: $200 per month

Medical expenses: $21,000 per month

Maybe, somebody can add up the cost to Medicare.

This times 310 million is unaffordable.

Jack LaLanne, *health and fitness guru, is proof—diet and exercise can prevent old age chronic diseases.*

But, there is a difference between eating cheeseburgers—and drinking sodas, habitually (or excessively), both contribute to obesity; but, one clogs the arteries: the other, is a factor in the development of diabetes.

The question with Bill Clinton: was he ignorant—or willfully violated dietary laws until chest pains and shortness of breath—appeared?

He was a cheeseburger and diet soda—junkie.

Some people—will drink sodas—like smoking cigarettes—even, if they know it is harmful. Therefore, a soda tax is fair—to pay for their medical expenses.

President Obama, probably, would be against the tax; since, he pledged not to raise taxes on lower income and middle class Americans. He rather pinch the rich to pay for their medical expenses.

The soda tax is a good (or better) idea! But, it has enemies: consumer backlash and beverage industry opposition—and politicians, like Bill Clinton—that serve both—not what is right—or science.

"This seems an absolute non-brainer to me," said Kelly Brownell, director of the Rudd Center for Food Policy and Obesity at Yale University who has long promoted such a tax. That is how I see it. The tax, plus—education—could prevent the 57 million pre-diabetes from moving into stage 2 diabetes. The American Heart Association says, "The biggest culprit for the glut of sugar, soft drinks by far....

The tax probably should be on grams of sugar—rather than ounces. It is not the liquid ounces—that is bad—it is the grams of sugar it contains. For example:

a 12 oz can of 7-Up contains 37 grams

a 12 oz can of Pepsi contains: 40 grams,

a 12 oz can of Shasta contains: 42 grams,

a 12 oz can of Fanta contains: 44 grams,

a 12 oz can of Mountain Dew contains: 46 grams,

a 12 oz can of Sunkist Orange Soda contains: 50 grams, etc.

The advantage of a taxing grams of sugar, instead of ounces, would reduce consumption and producers, might, reduce the sugar contents of soft drinks. That would be a double benefit.

It would be a good idea to extend the soda tax to other high-sugar junk foods, such as: candies and pastries, etc. But, I would start with sodas—to fight the diabetes epidemic and obesity.

Let's see what the 111th congress—does! Here is what Senator Chuck Grassley, the top Republican on the Senate Finance Committee, said: "I don't think it's going to have legs at all." If, the soda tax does not pass: it is because, congress thinks corporate profits and their campaign contributions are more important than a healthier America and funding healthcare reform.

Posted 9/3/09

ADJUSTED NET INCOME

I said, I would expound on this term in my new book: *The Tax Guardian. Com*—related to my Alternative Minimum Tax. I noticed: the Revenue Act of 1916—income tax rates were levied on net income. That term is no longer in fashion. The terms used today: gross income, AGI, and taxable income. The problem today: net income is decimated by exclusions, income deferrals, deductions, and exemptions: dropping taxpayers into a lower income tax bracket—than, they would be—if, the income tax was levied on net income. Now, the income tax is levied on taxable income. The expenses of individuals are treated more favorably, than the expenses of the government. Some people will argue that—citing reckless government spending, etc. The main reasons why people dislike paying taxes: the government wastes it, spends money it does not have for services and benefits, the tax code is skewed in favor of the rich, and not everybody pays their fair share. That hast to stop! But first, the people—must become informed.

I used the term to mean: all income subject to the income tax—after business expenses for the self-employed or entrepreneurs—plus two other deductions: the FICA taxes and alimony payments. I would apply my AMT on my model income tax table—to illustrate. I would allow all deductions, deferrals, exemptions, and credits in the tax code on the first three brackets. But, starting with the fourth: I would apply—the AMT—on adjusted net income—my second choice: AGI. The AMT would override the regular method of computing one's tax liability—if, higher.

If, you allow all above and below the line deductions, exemptions, deferrals, exclusions, and credits—in the US tax code; then, many middle class individuals—or couples: pay little or no tax—and the rich and super rich cut their taxes 1/3 to 1/2 on average. My AMT based on adjusted net income: would put a stop to these over generous tax breaks and deductions—that transform people into non-tax payers—or reduces taxable income to a mere pittance of net—or total income.

I certainly would not apply my AMT on income—on which, all or a big portion of net or gross income is eliminated by exclusions, deductions, income deferrals, exemptions, preferential treatment of income, etc.

In 2006, the top 400 earned an average of $263 million and paid an average rate of 17.2 percent. That is about 1/2 the statutory rate: 82.8% for the self—and 17.2% for the federal government is way out of balance. I believe—82.8% for the government—and 17.2% for the self is more correct: that would leave: $44.17 million for the individual. That is fair considering what the people, the government, and the nation's resources contributes to a person's income, profits, dividends, and capital gains.

I believe, my AMT is a fair and needed tax—based on today's badly designed tax code. My AMT based on adjusted net income is designed to counteract the growing list of above and below the line deductions, credits, exclusions (or tax-free incomes), and exemptions, which increases the number of people that pay no tax—or too little; so that, the government can not pay for the services and benefits it is providing—and creates a growing monster National Debt.

Therefore, a progressive minimum alternative tax, based on adjusted net income is needed. The present AMT—does a poor job.

It is not sufficiently progressive—it is complex—it has loopholes.

The AMT tax is 28 percent over $175,000—yet, filers with an average income of $263 million paid—only 17.2 percent in 2006.

My alternative minimum tax—applied to my income tax table—would be 55% over $23,356,932. That is fair considering the National Debt.

President Obama's tax proposals: does not come close—to solving the projected federal deficits for the next ten years.

Posted 9/17/09

Obama's Speech on Healthcare Reform—has Defects?
Revised & Corrected

His intentions are good—his strategies are bad. What he is proposing is not a national healthcare system: similar to those proposed by Theodore Roosevelt, FDR, Dingell, Truman, Clinton, Ted Kennedy, etc. It basically is an overhaul of the present system of healthcare provided through employers and private insurance companies—or HMOs; plus, it has a phony public option.

It is suppose to provide healthcare for the 46 million that are uninsured, can't afford it, private insurance rejects, the unemployed, etc.

Some things—the government can do better than the private sector and that is provide a national healthcare system for low and modest income people.

The reasons insurance premiums have gone up three times faster than wages: our medical care system is based on profits, overcharging, unnecessary tests, unnecessary surgeries, emphasis on treatment, not prevention, excessive executive compensation, etc.

Plus—our people are getting fatter and sicker.

Plus—the new methods of treatment are costly.

The government plan works on a different principle: it is a moral (or social) responsibility—to provide healthcare to those who are unable to pay for private insurance; like, the 46 million uninsured, paid for by taxes, and maybe, in government clinics and hospitals.

- 65 -

Unlike the private plan—since, its motive is not profit, it can put more emphasis on prevention—to reduce medical cost—and patient care over profits—and prevent unnecessary procedures and exorbitant charges.

After hearing and reading Obama's speech, it is basically, a plan to force the government responsibility—on the private sector.

Here are some of Obama's plan defects:

1. He said, "I am not the first president to take up this cause, but I am determined to the last." That is pure bunk: to be the last: his plan must be perfect. It is not. Healthcare is in a state of evolution and will be for decades to come. The Obama plan is in the Neanderthal stage of evolution.

2. He said, "Put simply, our health care problem is our deficit problem. Nothing else even comes close." That is false: our present deficit is the results of the Reagan and Bush tax cuts, the unpaid cost of the Afghanistan and Iraq wars, the Social Security $2.5 trillion paid-in surplus—that has been spent by the US government for the wars and other expenditures: plus the recession.

Medicare and Medicaid are not responsible for the $11.7 trillion federal debt we have now. That is ridiculous. It could be a future—cause of deficits—if, not handled right, particularly—his healthcare reform plan.

Actually, interest on the National Debt is our biggest future deficit problem, if the same trends continued—not including his healthcare plan, which he says will reduce the deficit. That is BS.

3. He said, "Well, the time for bickering is over." No, it is not. His plan is not the best plan. The best plan before Congress, might be H.R. 676 (single payer).

4. He said, "Now's the time to deliver." No it is not. The National Debt is too high—to implement a costly nationalized healthcare system—now. However, cost cutting improvements in the one we have are timely.

5. He said, "Under this plan (his), it will be against the law for insurance companies to deny you coverage because of a pre-existing condition." That may be, but that will drive up costs.

6. He said, "They will no longer be able to place some arbitrary cap on the amount of coverage you can receive in a given year or in a lifetime." How stupid can you get? All insurance polices: fire, car, life, casualty, etc.—have caps: no caps means higher risks and higher premiums.

7. He said, "We will place a limit on how much you can be charged for out-of-pocket expenses, because in the United States of America, no one should go broke because they get sick." I might add: he can not expect insurance companies to go broke—fulfilling his mandates.

The people have a false notion: that they can abuse health and nutritional laws for 20, 30, 40, or 50 years—and expect the government or private insurance companies to pay their medical expenses, regardless of cost, that is a misconception. Obama is nurturing that notion.

8. He says: "And—and I will make sure that no government bureaucrat or insurance bureaucrat gets between you and the care you need." He is promoting healthcare witchcraft. Don't be deceived—money will be a prime factor in the delivery of health care: public or private.

9. He says: "If, we do nothing to slow these skyrocketing cost, we will eventually be spending more on Medicare and Medicaid than every other government program combined." However, his no caps, no terminations, and no rejects mandates on healthcare providers will it make it far worst.

10. He said, "That's why under my plan, individuals will be required to carry basic health insurance—just as most states require you to carry auto insurance." What he failed to mention: the government will impose a fine (or tax) on your wages, if, you fail to purchase insurance.

11. He said, "Likewise—likewise, businesses will be required to carry basic health insurance—or chip in to help cover the cost of their workers." Chip in means—pay part of the premium or pay a tax penalty. That is tyrannical. It makes it harder for companies to make a profit. It puts them at a competitive disadvantage with foreign companies. It is not right to force employers—to pay for workers healthcare premiums on top of agreed upon wages—unless, the two mutually agree—or the worker takes a corresponding cut in wages. That is why the true public option is essential. It is a government run healthcare insurance plan [i.e., paid for by taxes]. He says: there are no taxes [on the bottom 95%].

12. He said, "Now, here's what you need to know. First, I will not sign a plan that adds one dime to our deficits, either now or in the future." If, that is the case, his healthcare reform plan, is dead on arrival.

13. He said, "Second, we've estimated that most of this plan can be paid for by finding savings within the existing health care system, a system that is currently full of waste and abuse." That is fine, but, there is a defect in his plan. And he said, "And this is also true when it comes to Medicare and Medicaid."

Not much can be saved in Medicaid, it is under funded. If, savings can be found here --it should be used to extend coverage. Make the savings first—then, extend coverage. That will solve part of the problem.

14. He said, "That is why not a dollar of the Medicare trust fund will be used to pay for this plan." Nor, should it be, but his plan does. He said, "The only thing this plan would eliminate is the hundreds of billions of dollars in waste and fraud, as well as unwarranted subsidies in Medicare that go to insurance companies." He cannot use money saved in the administration of Medicare part A [hospital insurance], to fund healthcare for the uninsured—or his public option. Let me explain: there are two different types of taxes involved here.

Revenues from the federal income tax can be used to fund any government department—and the savings in one, can be transferred or used in another, without creating a debt. But, you cannot do that with Medicare part A; because, it is funded by the FICA tax paid into the Medicare HI Trust Fund—and can only be used for senior Medicare benefits. You can borrow from the Trust Fund for other government uses—but, by doing so—you created a debt. Money saved in Medicare, part A, by eliminating abuse, waste, and fraud stays in the Trust Fund. He can only transfer money saved in part B and D—that are subsidized.

He plans on cutting tens of billions in Medicare Advantage, which is Part A, B, and D combined. And at the same time, he tells these people: "...don't pay attention to those scary stories about how your benefits will be cut...." Of course, benefits will be cut, if, you cut or end taxpayer subsidies. Let's be honest. Because, Medicare Advantage includes PPOs and SNPs, that is not going to be easy.

15. He said, "Much of the rest would be paid for with revenues from the very same drug and insurance companies that stand to benefit from tens of millions new customers." That is a bad design. They will raise the cost of devices, drugs, and medical care—to make up for the tax—or fee.

I believe this is one reason for laugher in the chamber of the congress; when, he said, "there remains some significant details to be ironed out...."

He did not propose one "dime" of taxes to pay for healthcare reform (i.e., for the uninsured). He will pay for his plan costing: $900 billion the first 10 years—apparently, by waving his Magic Wand—because, he proposes:

No deficits, no new taxes, no subsidies, no caps, no ex-extra charge for routine checkups and preventive care, like mammograms and colonoscopies, no rejections, no termination; a fine, if you don't chip in; you must buy healthcare, even, if you don't have any money, the government will finance it with tax credits—a decease in tax revenues. He is not being totally honest. He is like a 17th century traveling mountebank—going from town to town—selling miracle cures.

Where in his speech—did Obama mention the word: taxes—to fund his healthcare reform for the uninsured: there is none, if, there are: he is hiding it: he mentioned: tax credits. That is a government subsidy paid for by taxes, fees, and fines. Obama says, "But, they won't be." Does that mean to the newly created non-profit co-ops, the HMOs, or the healthcare providers? That is not lucid.

16. He said, "Now, if you 're one of the tens of millions of Americans who don't currently have health insurance..." Let's stop here: who are they? He says, "These are middle-class Americans." He distorts. They are the employees of small companies, who do not have employer paid insurance, the self-employed, the low and modest income workers with families, part-time workers, the high risk medical rejects, the chronically ill, people on welfare, the in-between jobs, some lower middleclass families, and people who can't afford medical care. How is he going to provide affordable and quality healthcare for these tens of millions. He said, "We will do this by creating a new insurance exchange, a marketplace where individuals and small business will be able to shop for health insurance at competitive prices." This is nonsense. These premiums will be unaffordable [i.e., for small businesses and individuals], the quality of service will be inferior, and the medical providers will lose money. Because, Obama says, it would be "self-sufficient"— "rely on the premiums its collects" and there will be no taxpayer subsidies. Read the speech.

Don't you see: this won't work? The Republicans do. This is what Obama calls: his public option. It is socialized medicine forced on the private sector, without government subsidies. The subsidies are paid to qualified employers and employees in the form of tax credits—less taxes paid to the government and refunds. Yes, they will help to pay healthcare premiums—but, if, employer sponsored health care insurance premiums more than double in the next 9 years, like they have in the last—while wages increase only one-third: premiums will become unaffordable.

17. He said, "And all insurance companies that want access to this new marketplace will have to abide by the consumer protections I already mentioned." They won't want to participate. Where in his plan: does he protect insurance companies or HMOs from drug addicts, alcoholics, the seriously ill, those that abuse their health, and game the system: demand life-long expensive treatment, e.g., those that have HIV/AIDS, since, they can not be rejected with a pre-existing condition. For this to work: the premiums would go through the ceiling or health providers will go broke.

That is what Obama calls his public option. It won't work. It forces employees and employers to participate or pay a penalty, forces insurance companies or HMOs to comply with all kinds of stringent requirements. And it provides no taxpayer subsidies. It is a badly designed—[fantastic] public option—doomed to fail.

18. He said, "And this reform will charge insurance companies a fee for their most expensive policies...." I can't believe he said that: this is wrong. He is referring to so called "Cadillac" healthcare benefits given to executives. The insurance companies are not a fault here. High-end healthcare insurance plans paid for by corporations—for executives—at a certain level, or in excess of the medium cost of healthcare plans—should be taxed as income. Did he--or somebody else write this speech? It is horrible. His plan to provide "quality" and "affordable" healthcare for the 46 million uninsured, high risk rejects, unemployed, on welfare, low and modest income workers and families; some smokers, drug addicts, alcoholics, and mentally ill without caps, rationing, rejections, deficits or taxes—is poppycock.

Here, Obama, the Magnificent, is revealing how his low-cost-high-benefit universal healthcare plan, will work.

19. He said, "And, it's time to give every American the same opportunity that we give ourselves." He is referring to the Federal Employment Health Benefit Program, which covers elected officials, members of congress, and federal employees. This won't work large scale; because, the government pays about 70 percent of premiums. That is lopsided. It should be 50-50—like Medicare. That is fairer. The government is not 70 percent to blame for people's health problems. Lawmakers have tilted the payment split in favor of themselves—taking advantage of taxpayers. Obama calls it "affordable insurance"; that is, because taxpayers pick up 70 percent of the cost. That won't work universally; because then, taxpayers will be paying for 70 percent of premiums for 310 million Americans—instead of eight. That would be too expensive. It would require—higher premiums and lower benefits—and secondly, because federal employees have a steady job, make good wages, and generally are healthy. That is not true of the 46 million uninsured Americans: many do not have a secure job, make good wages, and many are unhealthy. In other words: the top well, high paid, and employed are less expensive to insure, than the bottom sick, low paid, and unemployed.

Barack Obama is a quasi-con man.

In his speech: he mentions saving money by eliminating abuse and waste in Medicare and Medicaid: he failed to mention the FEHBP. Why, because, he does not want to be booed on national TV—by both parties. Government paying 70 percent of premiums and employees 30 percent is skewed. It favors elected officers, members of congress, and federal employees. They can afford to pay more—at least 50 percent. It should be no better than Medicare—or private employer healthcare plans.

20. He said, "It is a lie plain and simple—we plan to set up panels of bureaucrats with the power to kill off senior citizens." I would not put it those words; but, we will have a deficit problem, if we don't ration medical care based on what we can afford—or pay into the

system. Keeping people alive or prolonging life days, weeks, and months with feeding tubes, ventilators, and sedated in a hospital bed—or ICU costing up to $10,000 a day: does not make sense. I think it should be part of our plan—to terminate medical care -- when it is deemed futile, counsel and assist the terminally ill, who want to die. Obama calls the charge—that his plan would do this—cynical and irresponsible. I would call his plan: irresponsible and inhumane; if it does not.

21. He said, "And if we are able to slow the growth of health care by just one-tenth of 1 percent each year—one ten-tenth of 1 percent—it will actually reduce the deficit by $4 trillion over the long-term.

But, he failed to tell the people—how they can help!

Do you know—that 10 percent of our total healthcare costs are attributed to obesity. That this cost can be eliminated by eating less and exercising more—or maintaining a healthy weight. The reason, he failed to mention this solution: he doesn't know the facts—or because he wants to be popular—rather than scorned. He should appoint a Health Czar to teach Americans how to be healthy—how to avoid chronic illnesses, that nine out of ten seniors suffer, such as: high blood pressure, heart disease, and diabetes.

The cost of prescription drugs are about 72 percent higher for the obese—than normal weight people: add to that: hip replacements, lap-band surgery, angioplasty, etc. They should have to pay higher health premiums—if, they fail to lose pounds and conform to health laws. These things can be prevented.

Please—don't say it is genetics. There is no obesity problem in North Korea, where there is a lack of food. Kim Jong Il is proof of what over eating can do—the one fat person in the country—prior to his health problems: reported to be diabetes, heart disease, etc.

22. Obama said, "The public option—the public option is only a means to the end, and we should remain open to other ideas that

accomplish our ultimate goal." Senator Baucus (D-Mont) has come up with a different plan: replacing the public option with state-level non-profit cooperatives in which consumers could band together to buy private insurance.

That—might work in some places—and not others. It would save only about $50 billion over ten years: it is funded by a number of abusive taxes. I believe the public option—rightly designed—holds the best promise for the future. The question is: when, is the right time to implement? I believe it is also a responsibility of the people to bring medical cost down. Michael Roizen, MD and chief wellness officer at the Cleveland Clinic, states: tobacco, physical inactivity, food choices, and stress—account for 75 percent of our total cost of care. No plan is going to work; if, the people don't take more responsibility for their health. However, I am not convinced, the food industry and the medical profession want to change that. If, Americans would correct these four infractions: that would, seriously, cut into the profits of the tobacco, medical, and drug companies. They are all for: the government paying for people's medical expenses—as they develop chronic diseases—from their life styles.

In response to Obama's statement, he was open to other ideas: Republicans held copies of their plan: I took a look at it: H.R. 3400.

It does not require individuals to join—or employers, it gives tax credits to low and modest income Americans. It would also let dependents under twenty-five to stay in their parent's health insurance. It would allow states, associations, and small businesses to pool together to offer health insurance. It will reduce medical cost by implementing tort reform. It makes sense and cost less.

I prefer it—to Obama's public option—based on voodoo.

Maybe, we also should take a look at the British Plan: socialized medicine. That is better than what we got (i.e., for the majority). Instead of premiums: it is paid for by taxes. That might be the best plan. Those that disagree and can afford it—can buy private healthcare plans.

The British plan—has one big advantage: it lifts the cost of healthcare off the backs of employers. The Obama plan—puts more weight on.

Based on costs and benefits—the Canadian—single payer plan: does a better job—than, the US plan (i.e., for the bottom majority).

The question is: Is the Obama plan—superior?

No, it promises too much. Premiums from these low and modest income—no income, on welfare, high risk, (some) seriously ill people will not pay for their no-cap, no extra-fees, no cancellation, high cost medical care without subsidies. Obama's public option is not what Wagner/Murray/ Dingell—or Ted Kennedy had in mind—a new low-cost, high-risk Freddie and Fannie of healthcare.

Insurance companies won't want to participate. It is, mostly, under funded. It is highly regulated by the government. It is administrated by Obama's magic wand—you are required to do this (no caps) and that (no rejects)—and provide "quality" and "affordable" healthcare to these uninsured people without taxpayer subsidies, it will steal from Medicare. It has individual and employer penalties, if, you don't join. It places the burden of insuring the uninsured, low and modest income, (some) sick, and high risk people, on the backs of employers, rather than the government. The tax credits will not create deficits and, somehow, fees from health care providers and drug companies will help finance the plan. It is bogus— based on hope and bad math.

A true public [government] option—should be fully funded by taxes and the government would—either, provide care medical in its clinics, hospitals, and by its medical staff—or subcontract it out—to private medical clinics, hospitals, and doctors. I believe, it can work side-by-side with private insurance plans—filling in the gaps.

23. It establishes penalties for issuers of healthcare that fail to comply with regulations and no penalties for enrollees or patients that abuse their health: alcoholics, drug addicts, weight gainers, gay men, etc. Obama says: "We must be honest with ourselves." He is not—entirely.

24. Obama's public option plan is different: he says, no taxpayer subsidies. Of course, that is wrong. The transfer of savings in Medicare to his plan—are taxpayer subsidies. It forces issuers

of healthcare insurance to accept high cost, high risk enrollees that normally, they would not accept—without government subsidies—that will drive the cost of premiums. His subsidies are paid to employees and employers: called tax credits. He says no taxes: of course, that is wrong: employer and employee penalties that don't join and premiums are disguised taxes.

25. Obama says, the purpose of this national exchange is that: these 46 million uninsured—can bargain collectively—rather than individually and get better terms. I don't want to dampen enthusiasm for his plan; but, this group of all types, who join the pool—will be scattered in all 50 states: composed of mostly, low and modest income workers with families, some with diabetes, cancer, arteriosclerosis, arthritis, birth defects, HIV/AIDS, and other underlying health problems. Obama thinks insurance companies will jump at the chance to insure a slice. I don't—not under his rules: no annual and lifetime caps, no rejections, no terminations, etc.—unless, they raise premiums, reduce coverage, raise deductibles, etc. On the other hand, those that want healthcare insurance will not be able pay the higher premiums—or like the coverage. These higher premiums will increase government costs: tax credits paid to employees and employers. What, Obama is creating here: is a big subprime healthcare fiasco.

26. And, his plan—does not solve the problem of 10 to 12 million immigrants that are here illegally, which, he says: his plan excludes.

Oprah once said, "I am not voting for Barack Obama, because, he is black." [but] because, "he is brilliant." That is false. It's because he is black. He is not brilliant: he thinks he is brilliant. There is a difference.

His healthcare reform plan is based on magic solutions.

He is trying to force a national healthcare plan on the backs of employers and insurance companies. That is going to fail—backfire. It will force some employers out of business, increase unemployment, make it harder on others to make a profit, and insurance companies will raise premiums—when, forced to provide no limit, medical care for high risk enrollees. That will cause other people and employers to drop out—or balk. That is not the solution.

The reasons: we pay 1 & 1/2 times as much for healthcare, than any nation in the world and get less benefit—we are on the wrong tracks. Socialized medicine should not be a dirty word.

Britons prefer their plan [NHS] to ours.

Obama's public option also might work—if properly funded and the terms are modified. Proof—is in the pudding.

What will work—is—what people like.

Medical care provided by the private sector (or)

Medical care provided by the government

The third option: Obamacare—a chocolate coated healthcare plan with limburger cheese, nuts, aspartame, termites and maggots inside—or partially funded socialized medicine forced on the private sector.

President Obama is right about one thing: healthcare needs reform. But, I would make bringing the deficit down my top priority: that means: reforming both healthcare, the American people, and the US Tax Code.

Posted 9/25/09

Obama on Face the Nation (9/20/09)
Revised & Corrected

It begins with a quote from Senator Orrin Hatch (R-Utah), these are his words: **"If anyone believes that Washington can do a plan that will cost close to a trillion dollars, cover all Americans, not raise taxes on anyone, not increase the deficit, not reduce benefits or choices for our families and seniors, then I have a bridge to sell you."**

Schieffer asked: "Have you promised too much, Mr. President."

Obama replied: "No I don't think I've promised too much at all."

This answer: reminds me of OJ, who pleaded innocent of double murder—after a ton of evidence was complied against him.

What President Obama did—to defend himself: he used clever; but, false arguments.

He said, "Now, let me be honest:" But, is he right? Let me explain. This is a matter of polemics—or confutation. As he said, this is a complex matter and it depends on comprehension.

Schieffer said: "No tax increase on people who made under 250,000 dollars."

Obama: "right."

Schieffer: "....no tax of any kind on Americans. Can you still make that promise to people today?"

Obama: "I can still keep that promise because, as I've said, about two-thirds of what we've proposed would be from money that's already in the health care system but just being spent badly."

Now, let's stop here: two-thirds of $900 billion is $600 billion. He can't take from Medicare [HI]—because that is stealing, except for Medicare parts B and D, which are subsidized. He cannot touch the VA program. Congress will not, likely, cut FEHBP—their medical coverage. That leaves Medicaid—the federal-state medical program for the poor. That is under funded. The House bill: HR 3200—which embodies Obama's core principles, expands coverage. So, not much can be saved here.

He says: "the other third"......"Insurance companies, drug companies are gonna have to be ponying up, partly because right now they're receiving huge subsidies from folks." That is nonsense.

You can't pay for a $900 billion healthcare plan based on misappropriation, savings from Medicare, Medicaid, and ponying up by drug companies. They already have promised $80 billion in Rx price cuts. There has to be some from of taxation on those that receive the benefits. Obama said, no taxes of any kind.

RNC Chairman, Michael Steel, said on CBS: what Obama is proposing: no taxes, no deficits: is "unbelievable." I agree.

He is already short hundreds of billions of dollars; because, his means of payment—is based on assumptions, faulty thinking, and, partly, fraud.

I believe Michael Steal is more honest that Obama. He says: "taxes have to go up for the middle class."

HR 3200—America's Affordable Health Choices Act of 2009, which expands coverage for about 40 million uninsured and includes Obama's government run insurance exchange—does, in fact, include two new taxes imposed on the lower and middle class.

1. It is financed—solely by premiums, which are paid to the government in the form of a payroll tax, or directly to insurance companies—or HMOs.
2. It requires uninsured individuals to join or pay a 2.5 percent penalty based on modified AGI. That is a tax.

The premiums and penalties are taxes on uninsured people earning under $250,000. People over, most likely, would be insured. What makes them a tax? The plan is mandated by the government.

They would not be a tax, if, enrollment was voluntary—in a private plan. This is a government run insurance plan.

HR 3200—requires individuals and employers to join—or pay a penalty; but, there are no restraints to prevent insurance companies from raising premiums and they will. The three core Obama principles: no caps, no rejections, no terminations, will force HMOs to raise premiums, reduce benefits—cherry pick regions to offer healthcare, or they will drop out—or ask for government subsidies.

To counter this: the bill contains a public option. The healthcare providers will offer through the newly created insurance exchange—its healthcare plans—for the uninsured subject to the government rules, financed solely by premiums, and without taxpayer subsidies. This part is unbelievable. Because, the pool that is left, are mostly high risk, high cost, low income and modest income individuals and families, that can't afford private plans, and generally pay little or no taxes. His healthcare reform plan creates another big problem.

Premiums for low and modest income individuals and families would be financed with another individual tax credit—adding to the number of people that get the protection of the Armed Forces, the services and benefits of the courts, the schools, the welfare system, and pay little or no federal tax—or get a tax refund.

That is moving in the wrong direction.

According to Obama, two-thirds of this cost will come from savings in the present healthcare system.

I have already explained: you cannot do that—for the most part—not near as much as he is stating.

The other third—by insurance and drug companies ponying up—he ought to know better than that. New taxes are needed—or there will be deficits.

Senator Baucus, Chairman of the Senate Finance Committee, should know you can not transfer savings in Medicare to finance healthcare reform for the uninsured—it must stay in the Medicare Trust Fund. This is a big Obama misconception. Taxes must be raised to pay for healthcare reform; but, because Obama has made a campaign pledge not to raise taxes on individuals earning under $200,000 and joint filers under $250,000, that is a roadblock. To keep that pledge: taxes are being crafted on everybody—but, those, who receive the healthcare benefits: millionaires, surtax on high-end health insurance plans, annual fee on pharmaceutical companies and healthcare providers, etc. These fees will likely be passed on to consumers.

You cannot fund a National Healthcare plan—so, that Obama can keep his campaign promise not to raise taxes on the bottom 95 percent. You can't stick the top 5% with the cost: that don't receive the benefits. The higher marginal income tax rates—is the best answer.

But, is Obama being truthful—when he says no new taxes of any kind? No. He is basing his opinion on a misunderstanding—what constitutes a tax. But, the truth of the matter, most of these premiums will partly be paid by employee and employer tax credits—or by the states for those with low income or no jobs. States will have to raise taxes.

That is, because, most of the 46 million uninsured can't afford to pay healthcare insurance premiums without aid.

And, when Obama says: no deficits: he is wrong or dishonest. According to a recent study by the Peter G. Peterson Foundation: the bill will add $39 billion to the deficit from 2010 to 2019 and $1 trillion, when fully implemented, in the next ten years. I believe this study more than Obama. Even, the CBO—estimated a big deficit—until, they changed their mind. I suspect—pressure!

So, if, Obama is honest: he will not sign his own bill.

Truth: whether you call it: fines, penalties, premiums, fees—it all a form of taxation—to pay for government mandated program. And, when you say, no taxpayer subsidies: that is a delusion—the no cap, no reject, no termination rules imposed on the private insurance companies, will come back to bite the government, unless government health, preventive, and efficiency measures can significantly lower medical costs. That means: reversing the higher cost medical care—trend. Since, the enactment of

Medicare and Medicaid in 1965, the government has failed to do that. It needs to change its thinking.

Verdict: Obama is guilty of errors, lack of understanding, irrational thinking, false arguments, and over promising.

Posted 10/6/09

Obama on Meet the Press (9/20/09)

President Obama went on *Meet the Press* to pitch his healthcare plan. And, he laid out his core principles:

He is going to create an insurance exchange—so that, [uninsured] people can negotiate as a big pool to drive down costs.

Two of his other core principles: a cap on out-of-pocket expenses and make sure that no one is rejected for a pre-existing condition.

And, his other core principle: deficit-neutral.

And, his core principles—did not include new taxes.

David Gregory, host of *Meet the Press,* asked some really stupid questions; e.g., do you agree: most of Republican opposition to him was motivated by racism, that led to a long detour—waste of time. He should have asked him details about his healthcare plan. I would have asked these questions:

1. Do you think—heaping more taxes on employers—might inhibit rehiring the unemployed?
2. Do you back the soda-junk food tax?
3. Don't you think: that your no-caps—no rejects for pre-existing conditions—and affordable premiums—is trying to force 12 gallons of water into a 10 gallon container?

Instead, David Gregory asked him who he thought would win the World Series. It was a superficial, dumb interview.

He also did not see or mention the big defect in Obama's speech to the Congress, when he said, "Reducing waste and inefficiency in Medicare and Medicaid will pay for most of the plan." And, he said, "Now, much of the rest would be paid by profits from drug and insurance companies that stand to benefit from the tens of millions of new customers." This is faulty thinking. If, you impose a fee on drug and insurance companies that will profit from healthcare reform that is a kickback. That is the purpose of the corporation profit tax. Besides, the drug companies have already agreed to $80 billion in Rx price concessions. And, insurance companies can't make money, if, there are caps on out-of-pocket expenses and no rejections for pre-existing conditions. They will raise premiums.

The Obama interview was followed by Rep. John Boehner (R) house minority leader, and Lindsey Graham (R), senator from South Carolina, who criticized President Obama's healthcare plan.

Rep. Boehner said: "It's a big government plan that has 51 new agencies, boards, commissions, mandates that is going to get in the way of delivering quality care to the American people."

And, when asked: do you think the Obama plan is dead, he said: "I think it is." He sees it differently than Obama.

Sen. Graham said, "And when he talks about how to pay for it, that we're going to get $300 billion savings from Medicare and Medicaid, we've never done that before." That is about $300 billion less than Obama stated on *Face the Nation*. And, he added: "It's about the president saying something the people inherently believes sounds too good and doesn't add up."

That is true.

Let me explain this again, what the big defect is in Obama's plan not seen or mentioned on *Meet the Press*: you can take savings in Medicaid and transfer them to fund healthcare reform—but not Medicare, part A [hospital insurance].

Federal tax revenues from the income tax, the corporate profit tax, the excise tax, etc.—goes into one bank: the US treasury. Here savings in one government program, like Medicare B and D-can be used in another or (reallocated).

Revenues from the FICA tax goes into a different bank: the Medicare Trust Fund. Savings here can not be transferred to fund Obama's healthcare plan, unless you borrow—create a debt. Savings here: stays in the fund and makes Medicare more sustainable—or financially sound for a longer-time.

It is like, I give you $100 to buy things for me at the market: these things only cost $85. Obama wants to keep the money that he saved by buying cheaper brands and on sale, put it in his bank account, and buy things for himself. That is, basically, stealing. Sen. Graham says: "we've never done that before."

So, this money that Obama is counting on from Medicare to fund his deficit-neutral healthcare plan—does not legally exist, at least in part. He is short hundreds of billions of dollars for different reasons. He is either a bamboozler or does not understand tax and accounting principles— concerning Medicare.

Two exceptions: he can transfer money saved in Medicare part B and D, which are subsidized by the government. Part B will be difficult—once the "Doc fix" is implemented. Part D will also be also be difficult— because,—his healthcare plan increases prescription drug coverage. The leaves Medicare Advantage comprised of Part A, B, and D. Yes, cost savings is possible; but, not $50 billion per year—that is projected.

UPDATE

Here is the proof: Obama's budget for 2011 increases funding for:
Medicare Part B: $24 billion – up 11.1%
Medicare Part D: $7.98 billion – up 13.67%
These figures indicate there will be no significant reduction in cost by the elimination of fraud, waste, and abuse this year.

Now—can savings be made in Medicaid? Not, really! You can cut federal grants to states, but, that puts more weight on the states. Savings in Medicaid—since, it is a state funded program—mostly—would stay in the states. Here are other reasons: its cost will increase at 7.9 percent a year for the next decade, partly, because of increased enrollments and rising medical costs. That would offset any savings—from fraud, waste, abuse elimination. Plus, Sen. Baucus's bill and the House bill propose to increase funding for Medicaid, the federal-state medical program for the poor. So, Obama's plan to use savings of $500-$600 billion—in Medicare and Medicaid by cutting waste and inefficiency is, mostly, boloney. He is like a pitchman, knowingly, or unknowingly—selling a product that has defects and misrepresenting its cost to taxpayers. Now, it is up to the congress to pass, not pass, or change HR 3200.

UPDATE

In late 2010, they passed HR 3590 —the Patient Protection and Affordable Care Act. That is a similar bill that insurers 31 million and costs: $849 billion over ten years. Affordable is highly debatable.

Posted 10/13/09

Obama on This Week (9/20/09)

[corrected 10/14/09, 10/15/09]

Obama goes on *This Week* with George Stephanopoulos—to pitch his healthcare plan and gets trapped! He gets edgy, cuts off George's replies, and refused to admit he is wrong.

Stephanopoulos says: "Probably the most definitive promise you made in the campaign is that no one in the middle class would get a tax increase on your watch."

Obama: "right."

He admits he said—that. But, his healthcare reform plan does contain two tax increases on the lower and middle class:

1. Mandated healthcare insurance premiums. Whether it is a payroll tax or a half-breed, depends on whether the final bill contains a public option—and one enrolls in a government or private plan.
2. The penalty or fine—paid to the government, if the uninsured don't join—or purchase healthcare insurance.

Here is where Obama traps himself, he said: "But the first thing we've got to understand is you've got what is effectively a tax increase taking place on American families right now."

What is that tax increase? He said [when], "Health premiums went up 5.5 percent last year." He compares premiums to taxes.

Stephanopoulos replies: "That is truth, but...."

Here is where Obama cuts him off—he is in trouble; because, he insists that his government mandated healthcare premiums and penalties are not tax increases and attempts to change the subject, he says:—"just to close the loop on this" and he puts forth his four healthcare principles. But, he does not lose George—he wants to continue the dispute. The Obama plan currently in the House: HR 3590 and the Baucus plan does required the uninsured to join the plan—and a fine paid to the government, if one does not.

Stephanopoulos: "Under this mandate, the government is forcing people to spend money, fining, you if you don't. How is that not a tax?

Obama: "Well, hold on a second, George." He, then goes on to explain his justification for making healthcare insurance mandatory. That his plan would give, tax credits, set up an exchange, and do everything it can to make health insurance affordable for the uninsured. [But, that does not answer the question.]

Stephanopoulos: "That may be, but it's still a tax increase." Let me explain: even if, the premiums are lowered—the premiums, themselves, are a payroll tax, if paid to the government—a quasi-tax, if paid to private insurers, and the fine or penalty, if you don't purchase medical insurance, certainly, is a tax—a source of revenue for the government.

Obama: "No, that's not true George." And he continues to argue falsely, to defend himself. His defense: the mandate is justified, so that other people will not have to pay for visits to the ER for the uninsured, and it will lower the cost of insurance or healthcare premiums for all.

Stephanopoulos: "But, it may be fair, it may be good public policy...."

Obama: "No, but—but, George, you—you can't make up that language that that's called a tax increase. Any...."

Stephanopoulos: "Here's the....[they are cutting each other off, it is getting intense"].

Obama: "What—what—if I—if I say that right now premiums are going to be going up by 5 or 8 or 10 percent next year and say well, that's not a tax increase [it is not, because it is non-compulsory private insurance], but, on the other hand, if I say that I don't want to have to pay for you not carrying coverage after I give you tax credits, that makes it affordable, then..." Here, Obama's line of reasoning is incorrect. It doesn't make any difference, if he makes his healthcare premiums affordable with tax credits, taxpayer subsidies. That is not the point. The fact, his plan—forces the uninsured to join—and fines the uninsured, if, they don't: the healthcare premiums and the penalties, themselves, are a tax. Obama won't listen to reason, so George brings out a dictionary.

Stephanopoulos: "I—I don't think I'm making it up. Merriam-Webster's Dictionary: defines tax—"a charge, usually of money, imposed by authority on persons or property for public purposes."

That is exacting what his mandated healthcare premiums and fines are.

Obama: "George, the fact that you looked up Merriam's Dictionary. The definition of tax increase, indicates to me that you're stretching a little bit right now. Otherwise, you wouldn't have gone to the dictionary to check on the definition."

That is not true: he went to the dictionary; because, Obama is refusing to listen to reason and being mulish.

Stephanopoulos: "I wanted to check for myself. But, your critics say it is a tax increase." He is correct. He wants to make sure—that he is right—before making an attack on his credibility.

Obama: "My critics say everything is a tax increase. My critics say that I'm taking over every sector of the economy. You know that.

Look, we can have a legitimate debate about whether or not we're going to have an individual mandate or not, but...." [You see: he is trapped in a corner and trying to escape, but George won't let him.]

Stephanopoulos: "But you reject that it's a tax increase?" He wants to pin him down, before changing the subject. And, here, he gets his answer.

Obama: "I absolutely reject that notion." He is wrong, he is stubborn, he does not agree with the Merriam-Webster's Dictionary, he does not listen to reason, he says he is being falsely criticized, etc.

Stephanopoulos: "Let's go to Medicare then...."

This gives me another opportunity to explain: Obama's deficit-neutral healthcare plan is based on fraud.

The White House, recently, estimated: $500-$600 billion can be saved by eliminating fraud/waste in Medicare.

Stephanopoulos: "But if people lose their Medicare advantage?"

Obama: "What I have said is we're not going to take a dollar out of the Medicare trust fund."

I have already quoted: where Obama will use savings in the elimination of abuse and efficiently in Medicare to fund his government healthcare plan for the uninsured.

True, he is not going to withdraw money from the trust fund—directly, but—-he says: "...we are wasting hundreds of billions of dollars in Medicare that is not making people healthier." He is going to use this money to fund his reform plan for the uninsured.

He says to Stephanopoulos: "This isn't a radical plan." It is radical and fraudulent. I know George would ask, how? Let me explain: he says, the purpose of the insurance exchange is to bring healthcare premiums down for the uninsured—by bargaining as a group, but, because the insurance companies—must take individuals or bundles without the right to weed out high risk people—the premiums will go up—or coverage will do down.

When, Obama's healthcare reform plan is fully implemented—it will require a tax increase on everybody, except, Obama will not be in office. He is just delaying an inevitable tax increase on the middle class—according to him: families earning under $250,000 [and individuals less than $200,000].

The government sponsored insurance exchange is radical.

The public option, the government offering its healthcare plan on the exchange is radical.

Thirdly, imposing fines on individuals and employers that refuse to join his plan: these rules are radical—according to the dictionary: marked by a departure from the usual or traditional.

Obama's plan is also fraudulent:

Let's say: Obama is given the authority to administer the Medicare Trust Fund. He found ways of saving hundreds of billions: he wants to take that money and put it his bank account—to fund his program.

That is fraud (stealing).

Because, the $500-$600 billion, that he says can be saved—means: he is spending the Medicare Trust fund (i.e., for seniors)—at a slower rate—or more efficiently.

The hundreds of billions of dollars saved in Medicare eliminating waste/fraud—cannot, legally, be transferred to another program. He is mixing the money that is in the Medicare Trust Fund with the US Treasury. You cannot do that: consult a tax-accounting expert. However, you can cut or end the taxpayer subsidize to Medicare Advantage that Obama stated: was $17 or $18 billion a year—and transfer that money to fund his healthcare plan—or any taxpayer subsidy to Medicare.

In speech to Congress, Obama said: the unwarranted subsidies in Medicare would pay for his healthcare plan: here on ABC, he states: the $177 billion saved over ten years, "why wouldn't we use that to close the donut hole so that the people are actually getting better prescription drugs." That is not a tax savings. What he is saving in one place, he is spending in another. Neither can he use the savings for two different purposes: to fund his healthcare plan (i.e., for the uninsured) and to close the prescription drug donut hole for seniors. This is double talk.

Obama appeared on three TV networks: CBS, NBC, and ABC—to explain his healthcare reform plan—and got away with murder!

Posted 10/28/09

Obama's Budget Deficits Revised & Corrected

The Obama administration, recently, stated the budget deficit for FY year 2009 was $1.42 trillion. That is three times the 2008 deficit—or $4,700 for every man, woman, and child. What is appalling?—the public don't seem to mind. And, that is the partial deficit. The national debt from Oct. 1, 2008, to Sept. 30, 2009, increased: $1.78 trillion. That is the total deficit. The reason: not all government expenses are included in the budget: that is the deception. I first brought this to the attention of the mass media in 2006, 2007, 2008, and 2009—and they have not made it public. Why? They are protecting their Bush tax cuts, mostly on the rich.

The US government is headed towards insolvency: the interest on the 2009 National Debt is $383 billion. That is 42.4 percent of the $903 billion individuals paid in income taxes.

The reason it is lower than 2008: the interest rate on Treasury securities; i.e., T-bills, etc. are at a record low. The reason for that: the rate of inflation is near zero. And foreign countries are parking money in US T-bills to guard it against inflation in their currencies, but that won't last long. As we borrow more money to pay for our deficit spending and the world recession ends: interest rates will rise again.

During the Carter years: it reached 15 percent.

The US government is currently paying about 3.8 percent interest on debt—that is down from 6.5% in 2000. And, as the rollover of T-bills takes place (i.e., low interest maturing T-bills are replaced with higher interest T-bills), the cost of the interest on the national debt will rise.

We are now experiencing the lull before the storm. As yearly deficits accumulate and interest rates on treasury securities increase: this is going to be a double drag on economy. It could go back to 5, 6, or 7 percent: each 1 percent increase of Treasury yield: would raise the interest on a $12 trillion national debt: $120 billion—per annum.

The OMB predicts—$9 trillion in deficits in the next ten years: that added to the 2008 fiscal year-end deficit of $10.1 trillion: totals $19.1 trillion. Rising debt and rising interest rates—will lead the US into a debt trap. Right now, the debt ratio to GDP is around 82 percent: the highest since World War II.

It was about 33 percent prior to Reagan.

It is expected to rise to 100 percent by 2011. Obama's plan of economic redemption for the US: economic growth through deficit spending. It is, like, spending more on your credit card—than you earn. Any idiot can do that. It takes a genius to increase GDP—faster than debt.

Obama thinks—because, we brought the debt down from over 120 percent of GDP after World War II—we can do it again. But, the facts are different.

Franklin D. Roosevelt did not wait for the depression to end to raise taxes, like President Obama. It shows the plutocracy is still in control of the US congress: no tax increases on the wealthy have been enacted.

Corporate tax havens have not been eradicated—as Obama promised to pay for the middle class tax cuts. A Senate report estimated in 2008 that the US loses up to $100 billion a year in tax revenues to off-shore tax havens.

S 681 [110th Congress] – Stop Tax Haven Abuse Act—sponsored by: Sen. Carl Levin (D-MI)—of the four co-sponsors: three are Democrats: 1 Republican: this bill has yet to come to a vote in the Senate.

HR 1265 [111th Congress]—Stop Tax Heaven Abuse Act—sponsored by Rep. Lloyd Doggett (D-TX)—of the 68 cosponsors: none are Republicans: this bill has yet to come to a vote in the House.

This is proof—the US plutocracy kills [good] bills.

If, economic growth is lower than projected over the next ten years and interest rates on a growing colossal national debt rises—that will be devastating. The potential for future economic growth is less than after World War II. Here are 24 reasons:

1. There will be future energy and water shortages.
2. There will be increased foreign competition—after World War II much of the industrial capacity of Europe was in ruins.
3. There will be environmental restraints on industrial expansion in the 21st century --that were absent in the 20th century.
4. Economic growth after World War II was based on a higher fertility rate than exist now.
5. The US does not have the natural resources to support much higher population growth without lowering its standard of living: one in six—now—lives in poverty.
6. American's employment in manufacturing has fallen from 16.5% of total in 1987 to 10.5% in 2005 and suffered a job loss in 2006, 2007, 2008, and a steep loss in 2009: 51,000 in September.
7. The average rate of unemployment from 1946 to 1980: 5.1 percent: today: 9.8 percent.
8. The future cost of commodities (food), oil, and metals will increase—as world demand grows and supply diminishes.
9. Hyperinflation will reoccur in the next 10 years—if, right measures are not taken to control debt.
10. After World War II—the people needed houses, cars, appliances, TVs, etc.—now, they have them—except not paid for.
11. The paid-in S.S. surplus has subsidized the federal government since the mid-1980s. That will stop—shortly, and the federal government instead of receiving this subsidy—will have to pay off the IOUs. That debt now totals: $2.5 trillion.
12. The US had a trade surplus—until about 1977—and since then, a growing deficit. The August 2009 trade deficit: $30.7 billion.
13. The Afghanistan War has been going on for eight years—and the Iraq War for 6 years, yet there has been no tax increase to pay for

it. All presidents have raised taxes during wars—except George W. Bush. A war surtax would violate Obama's pledge not to raise taxes on the middle class. This obsolete pledge is hurting America.

14. After World War II, the economy grew an average of 3.7 percent from 1946 to 1980: in 2008, it declined .43 percent and 1.4 percent in 2009 (est.).

15. The top income tax rate was 70 to 92 percent after World War II until 1981: today: 35 percent.

16. The $72 trillion hidden debt—i.e., for public entitlements: Medicare, Medicaid, Social Security, interest on the National Debt, and government pensions coming due will put escalating greater weight on the economy until it collapses—unless rectified.

17. The national debt in 1946 was only $$269 billion. Today, the National Debt is $11.9 trillion and growing at the rate of $3.81 billion a day.

18. Since 1980, a greater percentage share of the nation's income has flowed to the top 1 percent—less to the bottom 80 percent. That is bad for the economy—e.g., in 1965 the average total compensation of bank CEOs was 24 times average workers: in 2007: 275 times.

19. There are a decreasing number of producers—or workers—supporting an increasing number of non-productive people.

20. From 1950 to 1963 – for more than a decade—corporations paid over 40% in taxes on income; since them, there has been a seesaw decline to about 15% in 2009.

21. If deficits accumulate—and debt reaches $19.1 trillion by 2019—and the interest rate on government debt increases to 5.3 percent: interest on the National Debt will cost taxpayers over $1 trillion. That will put enormous weight on the economy.

22. Healthcare reform will put additional weight on the economy.

23. Tax credits and deductions have reduced—the percentage of filers that pay federal income taxes.

24. If, there is another recession in the next 10 to 20 years—after our National Debt surpasses 100 percent of GDP—and interest rates rise—significantly, that could bankrupt the economy.

Remember what Ben Bernanke said in July 2005, when asked: if, there was a housing bubble burst or recession—would prices come down substantially across the nation, he said: "I guess, I don't buy your premise. It is pretty unlikely possibility. We never have had house prices decline on a nationwide bases. So, what is more likely, house prices might slow, maybe stabilize, might slow consumer spending a bit, I don't think its going to drive the economy from its full employment path."

"......I am confident, in fact, the banking regulators will pay close attention to the type of loans they make."

He is now Obama's Chairman of the Federal Reserve.

Conclusion: the Obama Administration is not doing enough to lower the deficit, raise taxes and put the economy on a sound fiscal foundation. First, you have to admit: the deficit is $1.78 trillion for fiscal year 2009—not $1.42 trillion. That is a difference of $360 billion. The US government should—give a detailed account what the off-budget expenses are and stop deceiving the American people. Interest on the "S.S. trust fund" is part of it, but, the rest—I don't know—and I doubt other Americans know.

Basically, it is a US government cover-up.

Furthermore; I believe, there should have been $100 to $200 billion cuts in government spending in 2009.

There is a lot of waste, fraud, and inefficiency in the federal government. I would begin—by restricting the use of Air Force One. I don't see the benefit of Obama's frequent ego-trips. He should reveal what it cost taxpayers to fly him and his family around the country and world. It should not be confidential.

For example, what did it cost taxpayers for him, his family, and dog for a one week vacation in Martha's Vineyard: including Air Force One, helicopters, two house leases for the Secret Service and White House staff, etc. (during the worst recession, since the Great Depression).

Answer: probably, more than $200,000. Air Force One—alone—cost $100,219—per hour to operate. Camp David, the presidential retreat, 70 miles from the White House, is not good enough for the Obamas.

UPDATE

The military, recently pegged the cost to operate Air Force One at $181,757—per hour.

His 9 hour flight to Copenhagen, Denmark, shows he does not have good judgment. This trip was for the city of Chicago—not the federal government. This trip was a big waste of taxpayer money.

A second, spare airplane always goes along: that doubles the cost: and First Lady Mechelle took a 737-800.

Grand total: 8,379 tons of CO_2 emitted into the atmosphere: total cost: the US government won't tell us.

Things, like the Blue Angels—should be terminated. The government is concealing the total cost of this program: six F-18 Hornets, maintenance, training, jet fuel, crashes, etc. Times are changing.

Each jet burns 1,300 gals of jet fuel—per show.

Last night, I heard on CBS News: Obama has attended 26 fundraisers and raised $27 million, since being in office. The problem with this: taxpayers pay the hefty cost to fly Obama on Air Force One accompanied by a C-17 cargo plane loaded with limo and staff vehicles, etc. I heard on the news—in September, he raised over $1 million at a fundraiser in Beverly Hills. But, he should reveal what it cost taxpayers to fly him and staff from the White House to Los Angeles and back: 4,588 miles. I believe it is a waste of taxpayer money, jet fuel, and pollutes the atmosphere.

Twenty-six fundraisers in nine months: add it up—and then add up what it cost, if this practice is continued for 4 years. I don't see the benefit to taxpayers—or voters. This is the business of the Democratic Party—not the federal government. Air Force One—should not be used to attend political fund raisers.

About half—the cost—is borne—by taxpayers of the opposite party: the cost to taxpayer: in probably, more than what the president raises.

Air Force One is too expensive, a waste of our non-renewable resources, and too damaging to the atmosphere for Obama to use as his personal taxi, party affairs, and frequent vacations.

Carter sold the presidential yacht; maybe, Obama should sell the Flying White House—or use only when it is a necessity.

Obama and Air Force can be compared to Alley Oop and his pet dinosaur that he rode: no longer sensible in this world. Here are 5 reasons:

1. Air Force One burns 5 gallons of jet fuel per mile
2. Emits 2.53 kilograms of CO_2 per liter=0.264 US gallons
3. It cost $181,757 per hour to operate
4. Add: Marine One, C-17 cargo plane for his limo, a second dummy plane, and maybe a jet fighter escort, etc.
5. Aug. 3, 2007, NASA predicts global warming will bring violent Storms and Tornados.
6. Obama has a caveman's intellect.

Internet video-conferencing is a lot cheaper. Duh!

I think, if one man, can save taxpayers $20 to $40 millions—a year: he should do it: or explain the benefit of his frequent trips.

Obama's flight to Des Moines, Ohio, to deliver a speech on Earth Day burnt more that 9,000 gallons of fuel, spewed about 86.4 tons of CO_2 into the atmosphere, and the cost taxpayers about $400,000 to $600,000. The speech could have made at the White House. This is an insult to Earth Day.

UPDATE I

April 2, 2011, at a UPS customer center in Maryland, he sad: "Real energy security can only come if we find ways to use less oil…."

My answer to that: He should have an office in the capital with a video-screen, where he can sit in one place and communicate with leaders in the 50 states and around the world—just by the click of a mouse. That is better than riding on Dinny—his pet dinosaur, blocking traffic, polluting the atmosphere, wasting energy and taxpayer dollars. He is not willing to cut back, why should anybody conserve or buy a hybrid. He waste more oil than any man on the planet.

UPDATE II

May 23, 2011, President Obama begins a six day trip to Ireland, England, and France on Air Force One—costing taxpayers an estimated $3,813,075 and emitted hundreds of tons of CO2 into the atmosphere.

The 2 day G 8 conference in France; probably, could have been done over the Internet by video-conferencing.

Did Obama waste more than 1 dollar: Yes. He began his presidency by saying: Every taxpayer dollar should be spent wisely.

This trip was 4 days pleasure: 2 days business.

Barack Obama does not look Irish to me.

And, there was 1 extra passenger on the plane.

UPDATE III

May 29, 2011—Obama visits tornado-ravaged Joplin, Missouri—that is the proof of NASA's prediction [2007]. And Barack Obama is probably, the biggest single human cause—and other related threats to human welfare or health, such as: heatwaves, forest fires, draughts, rising sea levels, ozone depletion, etc.

UPDATE IV

June5, 2011, the International Energy Agency reports—despite 20 years of effort, greenhouse gas emissions are going up instead of down....

The same with the US National Debt!

I would stop the billions of dollars of farm subsidies that goes into the production of high fructose corn syrup and hydrogenated oil used in possessed foods that contribute to diabetes, heart disease [clogged arteries] and the obesity epidemic. But, we don't. Political contributions from food firms are more important to legislators than the health of the nation.

I would stop abuse and fraud in Medicare—not to fund Obamacare, but to make Medicare more sustainable. I would stop coddling senior citizens. By their reaction to healthcare reform—shows they are spoilt to death.

I would redesign Medicare, part D.

Fraud in Medicare exposed by 60 Minutes cost seniors, they claim: an estimated $60 billion a year. The ease that swindlers received payment from Medicare by submitting bogus bills is gross mismanagement. But, the savings cannot be used for healthcare reform—as mentioned. Part A—belongs to the Medicare Trust Fund. It shows—you cannot trust bureaucrats or government entities. You not only need the power to investigate, but make the findings public. The government, generally, does not take self-cleansing action until fraud and corruption is exposed by the Mass Media and the public demands action—or riots.

It seems everybody from the President down to the Miami, Florida, Medicare swindlers are getting away with ripping off the US government. Its refusal to answer questions is part of the problem.

Fox News does not even investigate. In fact, the News Corporation, which owes Fox News, should be investigated: why, it pays such low taxes. I tell you one reason: tax havens.

Secondly I believe, there should have been $400 to $600 billion in tax increases in 2009—and go from there. Letting the deficit increase: $4-5 trillion during the Obama four years in office is national calamity.

The Maj. Nidal Hasan Case   Revised

He went on a shooting rampage at Ft. Hood: killing 13 and wounding 43. And, afterwards, when questioned by military authorities: refused to answer questions and asked for a lawyer. This is insane.

I believe the Fifth Amendment should be suspended in the case of a terrorist act—or mass murder, especially in the military: that prohibits us from pursuing the truth.

Guilt is not in question—here.

President Obama agrees with the law and believes there is never any justification for enhanced interrogation—or so-called torture, if one refuses to talk—regardless of the nature of the crime. This is insane.

Is hate for US's attempt to stop Islamic terrorism in the world—something US Muslims on the surface refuse to admit?

Does their belief in Islam—trump the US constitution and the bill of rights?

Obama says: we are not at war with Islam; but, Islamic sects are at war with the US and the civilized the world.

Islam extremism is behind most of the terrorism in the world, particularly, in Pakistan, Afghanistan, Iraq, Africa, etc. That cannot be denied. Pope Benedict the 16th is right on that issue. The Islamic reaction to the Pope's criticism: shows it is a violent and intolerant religion.

I believe, this is a case for denying the right of the Fifth, since Hasan is an Army officer and committed a murder spree against fellow soldiers. Obama thinks it is too cruel to subject a mass murderer or terrorist to interrogation techniques, like water boarding, to learn the truth. He is soft—when he should be hard. This crime does not deserve the right of silence.

What is at stake here: the truth.

Do Muslims subjectively hate the US and are waiting for the day— they can impose Islam on the world?

Extremist groups—have made it objective.

This is not to get evidence for conviction. He is 100 percent guilty! This is to get at the truth. The truth is needed to resolve these acts of terror. Does Islam have a secret political agenda for the world?

Killing and wounding dozens of unarmed soldiers—who are fighting for human rights in Iraq and Afghanistan—shows a high degree of hate— that has been festering for some time. When put to the test: fighting against Islamic extremists: he failed. He made his subjective feelings objective.

He agrees with the terrorists.

Therefore, he must answer this question: who was the mysterious person that visited his apartment—two days before the massacre—according to a witness: dressed in full Muslim attire. That is critical. He should not have the right to take the Fifth Amendment: there is no question of guilt. He plotted and committed the crime linked to his faith—a devout Muslim. Therefore, he is an Islamic terrorist. To what extent—he had help or encouragement from others is a big question and should be investigated.

But, our laws have blocked that effort.

His family hired lawyer has told military authorities: not to interview or interrogate him. This is unbelievable—how, we have handcuffed law enforcement. The Fifth Amendment was written prior to the model T-Ford. It is not up-to-date.

The Fifth Amendment was written to protect the innocent from being tortured into making a false confession. This is not the case—here.

Before, I would begin enhanced interrogation, if he refuses to talk: I would invite an iman—to talk to him—and tell him—his murderous act—is not the teachings of modern Islam and to fully cooperate with the military investigation—and reveal how you came to these conclusions, who shared your beliefs, etc. So, we can get to the bottom this crime.

This would prove—where mainstream Islam stands—or do they subjectively stand with Maj. Nidal Hasan?

Do Muslims want to create an Islamic state—denying the rest of the world: the freedom of religious choice? In many Islamic countries: apostasy—rejection of Islam—or religious conversion is punishable by death, such as: Iran, Saudi Arabia, Somalia, Qatar, Yemen, Sudan, Mauritania, and formerly—Afghanistan. That is evil—a violation of human rights.

Manuel Paleologus II, a Byzantine emperor, said: "Show me just what Muhammad brought that was new, and there you will find things only evil and inhuman, such as his command to spread by the sword the faith he preached."

That was his perception in the 13th century.

What is the truth today?

In all of more than 50 Muslim states in the world: there are some type of religious persecution in the form of threats, arrests, imprisonment—denying the right an education, work, etc. and forced to comply—to various Islamic laws: Christians and Jews considered second class citizens—or *Dhimmis.*

The USCIRF names 24 countries—for having the worst record for religious freedom: 14 are Muslim: none are English speaking.

In Egypt, for example, the Baha'i Faith is outlawed. Its founder, claims to be a prophet (i.e., after Mohammad). That is the worst type of bigotry. In Iran, Baha'is are accused of spreading corruption and imprisoned. Its creed is eclectic and mission: world peace.

In Saudi Arabia all citizens must be Muslims. The government prohibits the public practice of other religions. Bibles are strictly forbidden.

In 1923, Turkey became a republic or secular state. But, that is not the crux of the problem. It is the heart and soul of the population which is about 98 percent Muslims. There have been many attempts—to re-establish the Caliphate and there is vigilante—persecution. In 2007, two Turkish converts to Christianity were tortured and killed—their throats slit.

In Sudan, the Muslim northern government has conducted jihad against the Christians in the South. Since 1989, two million people have been killed and thousand more enslaved.

That is what the war in Iraq and Afghanistan and other places in the world are about: no religion, but Islam is valid. Mohammad is the last prophet of God, which is ridiculous. No book written in the 7th or 8th century: inspired or scientific is perfect. I am speaking of the Koran.

It is the religious book of today's mentally retarded: to believe—that God has only one name: Allah—and Mohammad is his last prophet.

Its exclusivity is based on ignorance. At the time of Mohammad, other religious documents were not in print or translated. Whether, legend or fact, it is said: Mohammad was illiterate: that makes sense.

UPDATE

The killing of 12 innocent people, 7 UN workers, two beheaded, and 20 injured in Afghanistan—for the burning of a Koran by a preacher in Florida—is proof: Islamic extremists are violent and wrongheaded people.

Maj. Nidal Hasan is one of these idiots. He believes—non-believers—or infidels should be beheaded—and he is a Maj. in the US Army.

I believe, therefore, the Army should have the right to question officers about crimes committed while on duty. That is reasonable, just, and necessary to get at the truth—considering the horrific crime he committed. Did he get his nourishment from the Koran? the Mosque? Or the secret Muslim brotherhood? And how pervasive is his sentiments—among Muslims?

Maj. Hasan took advantage of his rank, compensation, and religious freedom until—he was asked to prove his loyalty to America and its principles and he failed. He was a Muslim first: the desire for political power linked to Islam—the source of most of the terrorism in the world.

Therefore, the law should not block the Army from the interrogation of Maj. Nidal Hasan. There may be links—to others. Do we have an underlying—hidden Islamic militant movement in the US? Part of the motto of the Muslim Brotherhood is: "Jihad is our Way."

If, this is the case, there can be no peace in the world.

President Obama does not think so. He went to Cairo, Egypt, to apologize to Muslims for the US. He said, "Islam is not part of the problem in combating violent extremism." That sounds like something Mahmud Ahmadinejad, the president of Iran, would say. The 13 killed and 43 wounded at Ft. Hood—would disagree. Obama's opinion is not based on facts. Most of the terrorism in the Middle East, Africa, Europe, Southeast Asia, and the United States—is related to Islamic militarism—or extremism. True, Islam has a bright and a dark side. The war is with the dark.

Why would the parents of Maj. Nidal Hasan—hired a lawyer—and tell the military: not to question their son? That is the dark side.

Posted 2/28/10

THE DYSFUNCTIONAL CONGRESS
Revised & Corrected

Did you see Sarah Palin on Fox News—Sunday morning: she must be on some kind of I am smart crystal meth.

The second biggest nut: George Will—he said on This Week: "I subscribe to Milton Friedman's view that any tax cut of any shape at any time for any reason is to be supported."

The third biggest: the sweet talking televangelist, Joel Osteen, his Sunday message: "Don't have a critical spirit."

Now, back to the subject—politics.

Rep. Anthony Weiner (D-NY) says, the "Senate our enemy." I agree. It is the reincarnation of the House of Lords in England—that represents the landed aristocrats or nobility. The complaint: it has often, delayed or opposed measures by the Commons to such a degree that the Governments have been forced to make concessions which a unicameral legislature would have avoided. The same can be said about the U.S. Senate.

It has become a chamber: that is stacked with law-makers that represent the corporate elite, special interests, and wealthy. Fifty-one corporate senators can block and delay bills passed in the lower House.

With the ownership of the Mass Media by corporations and control of the Senate by these entities: American has become plutocracy—ruled by the rich—and the majority has lost control. And the recent decision by the Supreme Court—gives corporations more power to influence voters.

The constitution has given the House of Representatives, generally, representing the people, which now numbers 435 members, the exclusive power to make tax laws—but 51 senators can delay or block their passage and they do: that is the tyranny of the minority.

I believe—that abolishing the Senate and returning to a unicameral congress—would better serve the people. The senate does not serve the people, when it comes to tax laws and the regulation of Wall Street.

There are 100 senators, who are elected for 6 years and 435 house representatives, who are elected for 2 years: this design makes it easier for the plutocracy to stack the deck—and achieve their goals. In addition to these numerical advantages: the Senate adopted rule 22, the power to filibuster, requiring a supermajority—or 60 senators to pass bills. In other words: 41 senators can delay or block bills passed by the House.

Back in the 1950-60s, the filibuster was used to block civil rights legislation and labor law reform in 1978; since then, it has been used more frequently. In 2008, Republicans invoked the filibuster 139 times. I believe—it does more harm than good—and should be disposed of.

Senator Claire McCaskill (D-Mo) says: "Why, because Republicans in the Senate—the same ones who spent years kowtowing to George W. Bush—are determined to block each and every one of President Obama's initiatives."

The Senate is set up—so that the corporate elite, special interests, and the super rich can block House legislation (i.e., by the majority).

The Senate or Republicans have blocked, opposed, delayed—or altered the following House bills:

The soda tax to fight obesity and related health problems and help pay for healthcare costs.

The Senate Republicans have stopped the war surtax, to help pay for the Iraq and Afghanistan wars—a perfectly fair tax.

The Republicans shot down the millionaire's tax to finance Head Start, nutrition, deficit reduction, etc. (Mar 2008).

The Senate healthcare bill, killed the public option.

The Senate healthcare bill—substituted the surtax on incomes over $1 million—for a tax on "Cadillac plans" to help pay for it: opposed by labor, saying: they took pay cuts to get the benefits.

Seven Republicans senators—blocked Obama's freeze on discretionary domestic spending to reduce the deficit.

The House passed legislation to tax "carried interest" –the performance fee of Equity and Hedge fund managers as income, rather capital gains—Wall Street money has prevented senatorial action.

The House passed legislation: that makes the 2009 estate tax: retroactive to 2010: blocked by the Senate.

President Obama proposed a cap on the value of itemized deductions of upper income taxpayers at 28%: it would have raised $318 billion over ten years—and affect only 1.2 percent of filers. The Tax Professor said, that "flew like a lead balloon in the congress" and he concluded: "Evidently, the rich still carry influence in Washington." Considering the projected huge deficits for the next ten years, that is a perfectly rational and fair tax.

Senate Democrat leaders, realizing the 28% cap was dead, proposed raising the cap to 33% or 35%: I read on one website: "that got a cool reception in Congress, especially among Republicans," and no action has been taken.

Recently, the Senate rejected a cap on credit card interest rates: one, Republican voted for it—38 against. Currently, banks and credit card companies can charge any interest they want. That is not right.

In April of 2009, the House passed the Pay for Performance Act, in response to public outrage over "unreasonable and excessive" executive compensation; such as, the CEO of AIG received $25.4 million in 2007, Golden Sacks: $68.5 million, Countrywide Financial: $103 million, CEO of Lehman Bros made $34 million, CEO and Chairman of Merrill Lynch walked away with $161 million, CEO of Bear sterns received: $60 million, etc., but after almost a year: it has not cleared the Senate.

Last year, the House of Representatives passed a financial reform bill: no Republican voted for it.

Paul Krugman said on ABC, "They [Republicans] will vote not a single vote for any realistic curbs on Wall Street."

In 2008, $18.4 billion in bonuses were paid to Wall Street executives during a recession and 14 million unemployed—is proof: that something is wrong with our economic system.

The House passed a tax on executive bonuses opposed by Republicans: that died in the Senate.

The Senate in 2005—refused to increase the minimum wage: unless, Democrats agreed to repeal the estate tax.

Senate Republicans refused to increase the minimum wage in 2006—unless Democrats would agree to increase the estate tax exemption to $5 billion for singles: $10 million for joint filers.

The minimum wage which had not been raised since 1997—was not raised to $7.25 until Democrats controlled the congress in 2007. During this same period: congress raised its salary eight times.

Rep. Peter DeFazio, D-Ore, has introduced legislation taxing financial transactions: 0.25% on the value of shares traded, it would also apply to options transactions, and futures and other derivatives taxed at 0.02%. Wall Street traders can easily afford it, this money can be used for government regulation, and it less harsh than the sales tax consumers pay on goods and services. CNN money report says: This idea faces staunch opposition among Republicans.

UPDATE

It never came to a vote.

No Republican voted for the reinstatement of the estate [death] tax—repealed by George W. Bush—for the year 2010.

Its permanent repeal is a goal of the wealthiest Americans (i.e., with very few vocal exceptions): the top 10% of families with 469 billionaires owns over 71% of the nation's wealth. The bottom 40% owns less than 1%.

All 40 Republican senators voted against reestablishing PAYGO, a perfectly reasonable measure to bring spending under control: one reason: it would endanger their tax cuts.

The House passed HR 1728 –the Mortgage Reform and Anti-Predatory Lending Act in 2007 and 2009—it has yet to pass the Senate.

Going back to the Clinton era: not a single Republican voted for the Omnibus Budget Reconciliation of 1993, which added two higher marginal income tax rates: 36% and 39.6 percent. They said: "the biggest losers will be the working class."

Rep. Knollenberg (R) said: "President's economic plan is not a deficit reduction plan, it is a tax and spend plan."

Senator Orrin Hatch (R) said: "High marginal tax rates discourage work, savings, investment, and risk-taking. Taxes aimed at the so-called wealth always end up hitting the working man and woman.

"Moreover, Mr. President, it is highly unlikely that the revenue expected from these tax rate increases will ever materialize."

Senator McCain tried to defeat the bill—arguing: the tax raises were unconstitutional.

The Heritage Foundation, a right wing think tank, initially funded by Joseph Coors and Richard Mellon Saife, with billionaire Steve Forbes on the Broad of Trustees, is a foe of the estate tax and a friend of the flat tax, said: "If enacted, the Clinton tax hike will fuel more federal spending, destroy jobs, undermine America's international competitiveness, reduce economic growth, and increase the budget."

Fortunately, Vice President Al Gore broke the 50-50 Senate tie—by voting for the bill. No Republican voted for it.

Contrary to these phony arguments: it resulted in four FY federal budget surpluses—and the 6.9 percent unemployment rate when Clinton took office was reduced to 4 percent by the time he left.

That all ended, when George W. Bush took office: the Republican controlled congress allowed the Budget Enforcement Act to expire and he pushed through congress a series of tax cuts, mostly, on the wealthiest Americans, and the deficits begin to snowball to what they are today, a recession, and close to 10 percent unemployment. Republicans want to keep the Bush tax cuts (i.e., on the wealthy).

Rep. Anthony Weiner says, "Republicans are our opposition." The corporate elite has picked the Senate to stack the deck, mainly, because there are fewer senators and are elected for 6 years instead of two—and they possess the filibuster, that requires a supermajority to pass bills. Generally speaking, 51 senators can negate the vote of up to 435 members of the House.

Here is what Richard Trumka, president of the AFL-CIO, said: "From 1946 to 1973 in this country, productivity doubled and so did wages." However, "From 1973, wages stayed flat productivity continued to go up—and the amount of money between wages and productivity going up, went to the top 1 percent."

Robert Kuttner, the economist and co-editor of the American Prospect, said the same thing: "Wall Street is getting too much. Main Street is getting too little."

In 1965, the average CEO total compensation was 24 times the average pay for workers, in 2007: 275.4.

On top of this: the top income tax rate has been reduced from 70% to 35% in the same period, income from dividends, a major source of income of the super rich, has been given preferential treatment and taxed at 15 percent; long-term capital gains reduced to 15 percent, and the estate tax exemption raised from $143,333 to $3.5 million for individuals and $7 million for couples. I blame that, mostly, on the Republican control of congress.

During the Bush years, two-thirds of total income gains from 2002 to 2007 flowed to the top 1 percent of households: bottom 90%: 3.9%.

Here is the voting record of the Senate Majority leader during the Bush Administration—currently, the Republican senate leader, Mitch McConnell. He voted:

NO on increasing tax rate for people earning over $1 million (2008).

YES on permanently repealing the Estate Tax—pejoratively called the "Death Tax" (2006).

YES on raising the estate tax exemption to $5 million from $1 million.

NO on $47B for military by repealing the capital gains and dividend tax cuts.

YES on the Bush $350 billion tax cuts (2003).

YES on retaining reduced taxes on capital gains & dividends (2006).

YES on repealing the Alternative Minimum tax (2007).

YES on requiring supermajority for raising taxes (1998).

Rated 0% by the CTJ.

Voted NO on raising the minimum wage to $7.25 (2005).

NO on repealing tax subsidy for companies which move US jobs offshore (2005).

NO on $60 B stimulus package for jobs, infrastructure, and energy (2008).

NO on capping credit card interest rates (2009).

YES on congressional pay raise (2009).

Rated 0% by the AFL-CIO.

And this is typical of House Republicans; for example, here is the voting record of John Boehner (R), the current minority leader in the House—and was majority leader during the Bush Administration, replacing Tom Delay. He voted:

NO on increasing tax rate for people earning over $1 million (2008).

NO on paying for AMT relief by closing offshore business loopholes (2007).

YES on permanently repealing the Estate Tax.

YES on raising the estate tax exemption to $5 million from $1M.

YES on making the Bush tax cuts permanent.

YES on retaining reduced taxes on capital gains and dividends (2005).

YES on the Bush $958 billion tax cut over ten years (2001).

Rated 0% by the CTJ.—indicating opposition to progressive taxation. He is member of the Congressional Flat Tax Caucus.

Voted NO on regulating the subprime mortgage industry (2007).

NO on $60 billion stimulus package for jobs, infrastructure, and energy (2005).

NO on letting shareholders vote on executive compensation (2007 and 2009).

No on increasing minimum wage to $7.25 (2007).

Rated 7% by the AFL-CIO.

He recently said, "we're not going to roll over in our principles." These votes are the principles of the Republican Party. Mitch McConnell voted 92.9% with the Republican Party.

And, this was the complaint of President Obama, in his State of Union address: Republicans are saying no—"to everything." Richard

Kuttner on the Bill Moyers Journal called it, "Republican wall-to-wall obstructionism." It is not good politics—to work for the failure of a Democrat President—in order—to elect a Republican President in 2012. And, when Obama went to speak at the Republican House Conference— to seek bipartisan support: here is what Rep. Mike Pence said: "Mr. President, would—will you consider supporting across the board tax relief, as President Kennedy did?"

You see—to get cooperation: they want more tax cuts. That is their primary goal: blocking the sunset of the Bush tax cuts on the wealthy. They argue: tax cuts will create jobs. But, it did not work in the Bush Administration: workers got a small tax cut: the top 1 percent got a humongous tax cut. For that small tax cut—workers got a growing humongous National Debt.

What Obama failed to mention: circumstances are different now. Here are 4 major differences:

1. In 1961, when Kennedy took office: the top income tax rate was 91 percent. He cut it to 77% and to 70%. Today, the top rate: 35 percent.

2. During the Kennedy years dividends were subject to the marginal income tax rates. He did not reduce them—Bush reduced the top rate to 15 percent.

3. Kennedy cut the corporate tax rate from 52% to 50% in 1963 and to 48% in 1964. Today, the corporate statutory income tax rate 35%. However, the most profitable Fortune 500 companies pay an average effective rate about half.

4. In 1961, the National Debt: $290 billion: today $12.3 trillion and growing at the rate of $3.9 billion a day—since, Sept. 2007.

During the period from 1961 to 1980, when the top income tax rate was between 91 to 70 percent: the ratio of National Debt to GDP decreased from 55.1% to 33%. After, the top income tax rate was cut from 70% to 35%: the ratio of National Debt to GDP increased from 33 percent to 85.1%—today [2/8/10].

Conclusion: Senate Republicans—or Republicans legislators; mostly, represent the interests of rich and superrich—their refusal to raise taxes on the richest Americans for wars, deficits, healthcare, and other needs: is bad, wrong, and hurting this nation.

I agree with Bill Gates speaking on ABC—Good Morning—warned to reduce the deficits: "Taxes are going to have to go up and entitlements are going to have to be modified." That makes sense.

I also agree with Richard Trumka, he said on the Bill Moyers Journal: "let's look at who created this mess. The banks created this mess. Wall Street created this mess. And the super rich have had a tax break from Bush $1.2 trillion. We can take a little back from the rich that have enjoyed the last ten years in an unprecedented way, and pay for the creation of jobs that they actually destroyed."

To get out of the escalating Debt Crisis—-it is necessary to raise taxes, not a little, but a lot: the top income tax rate must go back to 70 percent, dividends taxed as income, long-term capital gains taxed from 15 to 35 percent, and the estate tax made progressive and the exemption lowered. And, I would hold off on National Healthcare system until the economy recovers and begin the work of reducing over generous government entitlements, such as: government pensions.

I would not hold off—on eliminating the $500-600 billion of fraud and waste in Medicare and Medicaid: that Obama says exists.

Here Obama is off-tract: he is recommending more entitlements, tax cuts and tax credits—during soaring deficits to regain his sagging popularity. That is pandering. He has criticized Wall Street—but getting tax reforms [i.e., higher taxes on the richest Americans] through the congress, especially, the Senate—as it is constituted now—is next to impossible.

Posted 3/1/10

Critique of the CHARLIE ROSE show:
Feb. 18, 2010: The Debt and the Deficit   Revised

He said, "The Congressional Budget Office recently projected that total debt this year would climb to nearly $9 trillion, or 60 percent of GDP, the highest level in nearly 60 years."

That is wrong; maybe, he is confusing it with the CBO forecast: the deficit between 2010 and 2019 would total $9.1 trillion. He is so far off on this subject, he is a moron. In 2007, the debt ratio to GDP was 65.5 percent. And, what is disturbing: none of his five guests: Paul Krugman, Nobel laureate economist; Alan Auerback of Univ. of Cal-Berkeley, David Walker of the Peterson Foundation, Rep. John Spratt, or Mohamed El-Erain of PIMCO corrected him—so, I will.

Here are the approximate correct figures: the National Debt on Oct. 1, 2009 was $11.9 trillion—add to that the estimated budget deficit for 2010 of $1.5 trillion: that totals $13.4 trillion: divide that by the projected GDP for 2010 of $14.7 trillion: that equals a debt ratio to economy of 91 percent. That is a big difference.

I agree with almost all of what his five guests said, except Paul Krugman, on one thing: he under estimates the seriousness of the growing National Debt problem. In response to Charlie Rose's question, "Is there an acceptable range of which debt should be as a percentage of GDP?"

He answered, "We had debt that was more than 120 percent of GDP, much, much larger, double where we are now at the end of World War

II." He is ill-informed also. It is not 50% of the World War II figure. It is approaching. But look—times are different: debt reduction is more difficult now. Auerback is right on this issue.

He said, the difference now, we are "facing exploding entitlement programs that we have no means to pay for."

I would add to that numerous other differences after World War II: we had high taxes, high employment, high economic growth, big oil reserves, bountiful water supply, favorable trade balances, little foreign competition, less gridlock in congress, and we had a Social Security surplus to pay for other government programs, and no or little environmental limits on economic growth.

Now, we have low taxes, big budget deficits, big trade deficits, high unemployment, oil production has peaked, we are facing water shortages, stiff foreign competition, rising interest rates, rising medical costs, rising energy costs, there are environmental limits on economic growth, there is gridlock in the congress, and instead of a Social Security paid-in-surplus to operate federal government, we must pay back the $2.5 trillion we borrowed. All of these factors, plus the growing mammoth off budget entitlements of Social Security, Medicare, Medicaid, and government pensions, which David Walker says totals: $60 trillion—makes debt reduction more difficult now.

Krugman says, "And while I hate that $60 trillion-dollar calculation, I think that is misleading, but the fact of the matter is, we were dead stuck on health care reform, on Medicare reform, on the long run budget issues before any of the things that Mohamed is talking about started." In my opinion, that does not explain why it is misleading. It is mumbo-jumbo.

Let's go to the interest on the National Debt:

David M. Walker says: "Even if they don't go up [interest rates], the single largest line item in the federal budget within 12 years will be interest on the federal debt—larger than defense, larger than Medicare, larger than Social Security. And what do we get for that? Nothing."

Krugman says almost the same thing: "I really hate that calculation"....."It's a very misleading number"....."we could handle it easily." I don't, totally, agree with that. I agree with Rep. John Spratt, he said, "I would like to say as a practical politician going back to net interest on the national debt—this year it's $188 billion, 10 years from now it's $720 billion. David Walker is right. This is a problem politically for us in the sense that I have to go back to my constituents and explain to them why their taxes have gone up to pay net interest on the national debt for what they see no real return that's relevant to them. That's a problem."

While I generally agree with that statement: the interest on the national debt is not $188 billion for 2010. It totals: $164 billion for the first four months: that could double or triple by the end of the year. I believe what Mohamed El-Erain, the CEO of PIMCO, the world's largest bond fund, says: "Worldwide we are starting to see a re-pricing of sovereign risk. Prices are starting to move. It is most visible in countries that don't have the ability to sustain high debt, Greece, were there's been a rapid increase in interest rates in what we call the sovereign risk. But also the United States. The ten year [bond] has now gone up to 3.80, the curve is steepening, so there's also a recognition that fast in some cases in Greece, slow in other cases, the market is starting to re-price the sovereign risk."

David Walker says: it is a "totally unrealistic assumption"—that interest will not go up. I agree. Look, if we add the $9.1 trillion in deficits to the 2009—$11.9 trillion National Debt—it will total $21 trillion in 2019. Let's assume interest rates will go no higher than 4 percent: that will cost taxpayers $840 billion. If, it goes to 5 percent: add $210 billion more. Now, I know Paul Krugman will say that is a misleading number. Here is why: it does not apply to all outstanding debt at once. It applies to new borrowing and refinancing old debt that matures at a higher rate. Higher debt ratio to GDP increases sovereign risk—which increases interest rates….

To answer the Charlie Rose question: "Is there an acceptable range of which debt should be as a percentage of GDP?"

One answer is this: according to the Maastricth Treaty, nations of the European Union's debt are not supposed to exceed 60 percent of GDP.

Wall Street bankers helped Greece shirt the debt limit by borrowing money by various derivative transactions, such as: a favorable cross-currency swap, which is not recorded as a liability—as would be a loan. Greece also hid certain gigantic military and healthcare costs, traded its right to future airport fees and lottery revenues for immediate cash, and practiced Keynesian economics (i.e., deficit spending to expand the economy), that worked until its economy contracted in 2009.

Today—Greece cannot pay its debts. On March 4, it refinanced $5 billion of old debt—at 6.38 percent. That is about 3 percent higher. More than $50 billion is coming due by the end of the year. It needs a bailout. Stronger lending EU nations are demanding: the implementation of cuts in expenditures and taxes increases. The austerity measures are driving the people of Greece to protest and riot.

Currently, its debt ratio to GDP is 113 percent. The US is not far behind and will, likely, exceed 100 percent by 2012. The CBO estimates: the national debt will reach 286.4 percent of GDP by 2050. Moody's and Standard and Poor's predict the US could lose its AAA rating in 5 to 10 years.

What has happened in Greece—can happen in the U.S. in 10, 20, or more years; if, debt increases faster than economic growth and interest rates rise—eventually, it could break the bank. Is it likely? No, if we fix the problem.

UPDATE

After reviewing my files: I discovered—I sent Charlie Rose a letter back in 10/31/09—stating the national debt, as of Dec. 26, 2007, was $9.146 trillion. I also sent him my book: **Why the Reagan and Bush Tax-Cuts are Unfair** (Second Edition), which explains the US government budget deficit—deception. The conclusion I have come to: he did not read it, disagrees—or is confused to believe or state on his show: Feb. 18, 2010, the CBO projected the total debt would climb to $9 trillion this year—or 60% of GDP.

I was perturbed, because this is not true—and I informed him of the truth—beforehand. So, I sent him this email:

3/15/10.

Dear Charlie Rose,

I wrote an article about you on my blog: thetaxguardian.com—concerning your show: Feb. 18, 2010: The Debt and the Deficit. I stated you were a moron on the subject and gave the reason. What is your defense or explanation? I will post your answer on my blog.

Now, I want to remind you—you said total debt—not public debt. There is a difference. If, you subtract the $4 trillion of intra-governmental debt; then, the public debt is about $9 trillion. That is a misleading figure. The US government, like Greece, is masking the size of its national debt.

The figures you quoted: does not include the $2.6 trillion it borrowed (or raided) from the two Social Security Trust Funds and other off-budget debt. That is deception. Yahoo News, just recently, reported: $29 billion of those IOUs will come due this year: that is not included in the public debt. It should be, because, taxpayers are on the hook for it. But, you did not use the term public debt. You used the term: total debt, which includes intra-governmental debt.

Are you confused, misinformed, or what? The reason I sent you my book and letter, so you would inform the public of the truth, you failed in that mission also.

What is your excuse?

Walter F. Picca

I have not received a reply—as of July 1, 2011.

Posted 3/22/10

THE HEALTHCARE REFORM BILL [amended 3/28/10]

Revised & Corrected

The biggest scammer on television: Sunday, March the 14th, was televangelist Joseph Prince. He says, the blood of Jesus has fully paid for all your sin debts. I consider this to be white bread, rather than whole grain bread (truth). White bread is more popular than, whole grain—because, people won't buy it—unless they like it—or it sounds good, or they are getting something for nothing. The reason I mentioned this: what is true in religion is true in the market place and politics—or government entitlements.

I am referring to Obama's healthcare reform plan: to sell to the people: it is misrepresented—just like the Bush tax cuts. Don't get me wrong: I think a national healthcare system is necessary and good, but it has to be designed right—or it won't work --or cost too much. Here are some of the misrepresentations—or embellishments.

Obama says, it will reduce the deficit by $138 billion the first ten years: that is deceptive, because it excluded the "doc fix" necessary to bring Medicare payments to physicians up to actual cost; otherwise, Medicare faces a meltdown: physicians will opt out—or limit the number of patients. The $371 billion estimated cost over ten years was placed in other legislation to make the Healthcare reform bill appear deficit reducing. The reason it was excluded: Obama promised not to sign any healthcare bill that would increase the deficit "one dime." That is hiding the true cost—or deception.

Obama says, his plan is deficit neutral: that is smoke and mirrors. If, you cut $500 billion in fraud and waste in Medicare—that reduces the federal deficit $500 billion. To use the same money: to fund Obamacare—you add $500 billion back to the federal deficit.

The $500/$600 billion—is a mirage.

Obama says [his plan], it will bring premiums down: it might for some and raise it for others. Premiums are only part of the cost; if, co-payments and deductibles are raised: there is no savings.

Obama says, no cuts in Medicare benefits: that is not exactly true: cutting the subsidy to Medical Advantage $130 billion: will shrink coverage [or raise premiums and co-pays].

Obama says, medical care is a right; not if, you are to blame for your injuries and diseases. It is an unmerited gift.

Here are some of the bill's other defects:

It lacks death panels: cutting medical care—when it is deemed futile—to appease irrational people—like Sarah Palin.

I believe, this money could be better spent by putting it in a fund—to eliminate or correct birth defects.

Dr. Kevorkian can help here—to reduce cost and end pain. He should be given the Presidential Medal for Merit—not put in jail.

The bill lacks a public option—an alternative—to rising private healthcare costs—analogous to a spare tire, when taking a trip, favored by the majority of people—in various polls. This sentiment is not reflected in the bill passed by the Senate.

The Obama healthcare bill is part real—part fantasy—the projected $1.2 trillion deficit reduction from 2020 to 2029. No man can see that far ahead: he was wrong—in the projected budget deficit for 2010.

The no cap—no rejection—no termination, etc.—imposed on private healthcare insurers: will drive up costs.

The mandate for employers with more than 50 employees—to provide medical coverage—or pay a fine of $2,000 per employee would put a brake on economic growth and new hiring.

The U.S. government is pilling more and more taxes on employers:

The 6.25% Social Security tax
The 1.45% Medicare tax

State and federal unemployment tax

Corporate income tax

Healthcare coverage for employees—or fines.

The danger: all these taxes may be raised in the future—as cost of these programs increase.

Companies are like horses, the more weight you put on them: the slower they run—the weak collapse.

The Obama bill highly regulates insurance companies and imposes no responsibility on people to cut medical costs, such as: stop smoking, exercise, prevent weight gain, eat right, etc.

Dr. Roizner states: 40% of all medical cost results from inactivity, tobacco, and food choices. Prevent a heart attack: save $50,000.

In car insurance premiums go up, if people get into accidents and get tickets for traffic violations: that should apply to medical insurance.

If, people smoke, drink excessive, use harmful drugs, eat too much, and abuse their health: they should have to pay more for healthcare—or be denied, or assigned to a high risk pool with rules.

Obama's bill is subsidized medical care for those that practice unsafe sex. HIV medications cost more—than, most people are worth to society – according to Dr. Michael Kolber: cost $14,000 to $21,000 a year: $400,000 or more lifetime. There are about 40,000 new cases annually: 47% black, 45% MSM. Blacks or African-Americans are 12.9% of total population.

Do you see; why, insurance companies—might want to reject people with pre-existing conditions—or terminate people with new acquired diseases. This is just one part of the whole picture—of higher costs.

Obama's bill contains no requirements for people to get off prescription drugs—by making life-style changes, where it is possible.

If, life-style changes—makes it possible for you to get off of prescription drugs and you refuse; then, you should pay for your prescriptions.

You want to smoke, (over) drink, take harmful drugs, gain weight, do not exercise, eat junk food—do dangerous things and are at fault for your medical conditions and injuries; then, you should pay for your medical care. Why, should other people pay for it?

The people who like this bill are those that don't pay for it—those that don't like this bill are those that pay for it.

When the government pays for or subsidizes your medical care—then, it has the right to set the rules. When, you pay for your medical care; then, you can do what you want.

Government paid healthcare should require people to maintain a certain weight—or pay extra. According to Humana, one of the biggest healthcare providers—each extra pound cost: $19.39 per year: do the math. If, the present trend continues: 40% of U.S. will be obese by 2018 and cost $344 billion in healthcare.

Solution: simply, eat less....

Obama's bill does not require food producers to take unhealthy foods off the market or tax junk foods and sodas to pay for medical costs.

From 1950 to 1990—the number of filers that paid no income tax—averaged 21%—in 2008—43.4%—Obama's healthcare plan would push that number close to or pass 50%.

Obama's healthcare reform bill does not sufficiently tackle the $38 trillion Medicare unfunded entitlements for the next 75 years—and increased the subsidy for part D, prescription drugs.

Medicare was supposed to be—pay-as-you-go, but that is no longer true. The projected deficit for Part A & B: $603 billion for the next ten years. The Medicare HI Trust Fund will be exhausted by 2017.

Part B—supplemental medical insurance—doctor's fees and outpatient medical costs, etc. is partly paid by premiums and government subsidies.

Part C – Part A and B combined.

Part D—prescription drugs coverage partly paid by premiums and government subsidies.

- Medicare Advantage part: A, B, and D –combined.

HR 3590—Section 10907 increases the Medicare payroll tax .9% for individual taxpayers earning over $200,000 and $250,000 for couples filing joint returns. This design is wrong: the bottom 95% of the people cannot expect to abuse their health: 20, 30, 40 years and expect the top 5% to pay for their chronic diseases, when old. This is Obama's campaign promise. It is unfair and discriminatory. The same Medicare payroll tax should go up the income ladder from bottom to top—without skipping rungs—to fully fund Medicare Part A—hospital insurance. But, Part A is not the immediate problem: it has a surplus until 2017. Part B and D have a funding problem: about 75 percent subsidized by the federal government.

The Franklin Plan

To solve the Medicare deficit: I would levy a 5% to 10% surtax on the income [including dividends, capital gains, and annuities] of individuals earning over $12,500 beginning at age—sixty-five.

I would combine A, B, and D into one Trust Fund: I can't see how you can separate hospital, doctors, prescription drugs, and outpatient costs: I would use the Medicare payroll tax and the senior citizens surtax, and premiums to fund the Medicare ABD Trust Fund and have two options: fee-for-service—or HMO plans. I would add a third: government operated clinics and hospitals—if, the first two: proved unsatisfactory: poor quality and high cost.

I would put a vote to senior citizens: do you want a higher Medicare tax or lower benefits? Seniors are responsible for their chronic diseases, for the most part, and they should pay for it.

I would put a cap on total medical cost per person after sixty-five: based on what is paid in the ABD Trust Fund.

Here are five options:

1. Conform to health laws to avoid chronic diseases
2. Exceed the cap by using your resources
3. Buy extra-medical coverage to bump up the cap
4. Let Nature take its course.
5. Euthanasia [where legal], if life is unbearable.

The Medicare deficit should be reduced to zero: by cutting benefits, higher premiums, the Medicare surtax, life-style changes, setting reasonable caps, and eliminating fraud, waste, and abuse. Passing the cost to future generations is wrong. That is like, renting an apartment—and having to pay the un-paid rent of the previous renter. It is not going to be easier in the future: less will be paying for more.

I believe the U.S. government is using unsound accounting procedures to fund Obama's healthcare plan.

I believe treating Obama care and Medicare, separately, is more responsible. The motive for reducing $500 billion of waste and fraud in Medicare—should be to make it more affordable for those that pay the Medicare tax, premiums and co-pays—as well as—reduce its [deficit] funded by the government.

The government says: the Medicare subsidies to B and D are paid by general tax revenues. That is not totally true. It is partly, or all borrowed money that is added to the National debt.

The federal government was operating at a deficit—when, these programs were added: therefore, their cost have added to the National Debt.

Likewise, the new healthcare program to insure the 31 million uninsured should be fully funded by new taxes; otherwise, you create a new $500 billion 10 year deficit—i.e., Medicare's deficit transferred to Obamacare and that will skyrocket when fully implemented in the future.

Also, there is a flaw in this transfer of money from Medicare to Obamacare. The money saved in reducing waste and fraud in Medicare, Part A [hospital insurance]—cannot be transferred; because, it is funded by the FICA Medicare HI payroll tax: you can transfer money saved only in parts of Medicare—funded by government subsidies.

The Obama healthcare reform bill did not correct the Medicare problem, part B and D—and created a new entitlement program.

The waste and fraud in Medicare should be eliminated, regardless of whether you enact a new healthcare bill. It should have been done—years ago.

The Social Security Act of 1935, which enacted retirement benefits for seniors, was funded by the Social Security payroll tax.

The Social Security Act of 1965, which enacted Medicare for seniors, was funded by the Medicare payroll tax.

The Obama Healthcare Reform Act of 2010, which is enacted to provide medical care for the uninsured, is two-thirds funded by reducing waste and fraud in Medicare. That is a gimmick—as well as fraud, if, they are counting savings from Part A [hospital insurance].

In 1930, the government paid only 14% of citizens' medical costs; today, it has gone overboard—53% of all health care is publicly financed in 2009—62% including tax breaks: not counting Obamacare. It must raise taxes—and ration medical care—to stay solvent.

Government sponsored healthcare insurance should have caps—like auto insurance and different plans: basic, middle, and premium. Coverage should be based on what the people pay in taxes and premiums.

Obama will insure 31 million uninsured people without the bottom 95 percent paying additional taxes: that is a scam.

Obama said, "your employer, it's estimated, would see premiums fall by as much as 3,000 percent [he meant: $3,000], which means they could give you a raise." That is unlikely [or a joke].

Larry Levitt of the Kaiser Family Foundation says, "There is no question premiums are still going to keep going up."

The benefit of collective bargaining on the exchange—will be offset—by new costly requirements on healthcare providers; e.g., no denial for preexisting conditions, no terminations, no annual and lifetime caps, and no rescission of coverage.

Because, there is no cap on premiums: people will be forced to pay; whatever, insurance companies charge.

If, you want lower medical cost: you must be willing to do four things: stop smoking, exercise, get rid of extra pounds, and eat right. Several more could be added to the list: wear a seatbelt, don't over drink, refrain from using dangerous drugs, and live a moral-religious life.

You want unlimited healthcare paid for by the government; then, you must be honest about the cost—and pay for it.

Do you see why white bread—low [or no] cost medical care—is more popular, than, whole grain bread: the whole truth.

Medicare, a big U.S. deficit problem, could be fixed by reducing benefits and enacting a surtax on retirement income at a rate that would be raised or lowered to maintain the deficit near zero. Seniors could afford it—by eating less and reducing medical costs. That is fair, because, medical cost rise as people get older. Seniors can cut their medical cost by life-style changes. I would not increase the Medicare tax—on employers.

People are to blame for their chronic diseases—more than the government or employers. They should bear most of the cost.

I would qualify that statement—on average—not, in all cases. All three are jointly responsible; but, the individual can make the most difference in his or her health. Experts agree: most chronic diseases: heart, diabetes, pulmonary, and some cancers, the most costly, are preventable.

If, you pay the cost of your medical care; then, it is between you and your doctor. However, if the government pays the cost: it has the right to dictate the terms—or the taxpayers.

People are like cars—sometimes—not worth fixing.

The major sources of funding for the 31 million uninsured—costing $849 billion in the next ten years comes from:

$52 billion employer fines, who don't offer coverage
$17 billion employee fines, who don't buy insurance
$60 billion annual fee on health care providers
$32 billion tax on "Cadillac" insurance plans
$27 billion fee on mfg. and importers of drugs
$20 billion 2.3% tax on mfg. and importers of medical devices
$15 billion changes in medical expense deductions
$2.7 billion 10% on tanning solons
$25.2 billion all other sources

> Bear in mind: the new .9% Medicare tax on high incomers cannot be used to fund Obamacare—that goes into the Medicare HI Trust Fund.

That totals: $250.9 billion: the remainder of money comes from the reductions in the cost of Medicare. That would be a legitimate transfer of money, if the federal subsidies to Medicare were funded by taxes; unfortunately, they are not—at least in part or all. So, what is being transferred to Obamacare is Medicare's deficit financing—not tax revenues. The reason this all sounds like double talk: Obama combined two healthcare programs: Medicare and Obamacama (i.e., for the 31 million uninsured) into one healthcare reform plan—or mixed the finances, instead of treating each one separately, which would have been more correct. Basically, some of government subsidies to healthcare should come from the general fund; mainly, the individual and corporate income tax.

The reason for these gimmick taxes: Obama promised not to raise taxes on individual earning less than $200,000 and couples: $250,000. This was a vote getting strategy to get elected. It is blocking responsible tax reform.

His hands are tied and the deficit for 2009 and 2010 is going through the roof. Cost cutting and tax reform should have been the first priority along with jobs and then, healthcare reform. Once the Federal Debt-Crisis is solved. Then, we can begin work on Universal Healthcare. It is affordable if the people will do four things—better: 5, 6, 7, and 8.

Posted 4/13/10

OBAMACARE FAUX-FUNDING Revised & Corrected

When David Walker, the former head of the GAO and Comptroller General of the U.S. and current CEO of the Peter G. Peterson Foundation, was asked by Aaron Task of Yahoo News, critics say: there is double counting in the healthcare legislation. He answered, the $500 billion of Medicare cost reductions—to help pay for healthcare for the uninsured is misleading, "but, I don't think there is double counting."

On this subject: the US government has not been forthright: stating specifically—what parts of Medicare, this alleged $500 billion in waste and fraud is coming from: this remains a Big Mystery.

You cannot transfer money saved from reducing waste and fraud in Medicare part A, which covers a wide range of hospital and medical costs; because, it is funded by the payroll Medicare tax—not taxpayer subsidy. It belongs to the HI trust fund. Savings in waste and fraud in this part means: it is exhausted at a slower rate. You can transfer only money that comes from tax subsidies. The $500 billion saving from reducing waste and fraud must come from Medicare parts: B and D: they are partly funded by taxpayer subsidies.

The question is: can $500 billion in waste and fraud be eliminated in these two parts—or will the cost savings be offset by increasing costs in the next decade. HR 3950 increases funding for Part D [prescription drug coverage]. So, I question: whether this is possible.

But, if it is possible—you cannot use the $500 billion in fraud and waste elimination to reduce cost of Medicare—and use the same money to pay for the cost of Obamacare for the uninsured: that is double counting—or posting two credits on the books: one is a debit. I don't think the CBO would be that dumb. That would be detected. But, the transfer of Medicare funding is misleading; because, it is not a transfer of tax revenues--but, all or partly a transfer of borrowed money [debt]—and part of the money is not legally transferable.

I don't know what parts of Medicare: the $500 billion in savings comes from by reducing fraud, abuse, and waste, because, the government has not told us. That part of the puzzle is missing.

Cutting the cost of Medicare $500 billion by reducing waste, fraud, and inefficiency over the next ten years is also problematic. Will or can the government do it?

Is the $500 billion fact or fiction?

The only legitimate funding of Obamacare are the new taxes, fees, and fines, mentioned in HR 3950.

The most egregious tax to fund Obamacare is the 40% excise tax on so-called "Cadillac" high-end insurance policies on every dollar that exceeds $10,200 for individuals and $27,500 for families. That is outrageous: more than the 10% luxury tax on non-essentials, such as: boats, furs, jewelry, and perfumes—that was repealed. Since, these policies are forms of compensation: over these levels should be taxed as income.

This tax is punitive—not fair. It is higher than, what would be paid, if these amounts were taxed as income. Because, it taxes the insurer rather than the insured: does not make it a fair tax.

David Walker says: his reason for thinking there is no double counting: the CBO is a nonpartisan agency—comprised of very capable professionals, and he knows the head of the CBO, a person of unquestioned integrity, and these people do their job, to the best of their ability. Maybe, there is no double counting; but, there could be manipulation of figures—to achieve certain results: make the plan appear deficit-neutral. By the way, the head of the CBO is Douglas Elemendorf, I question his integrity. He is under the Speaker of the House, Nancy Pelosi.

The 2010 - 2019 projected cost of Medicare: $6.4 trillion. I believe the U.S. government—should give taxpayers a clear picture: how much is funded by the payroll Medicare tax, by premiums, and how much by deficit financing [subsidies]—and how much of the $500 billion in savings—or reduced costs: will come from part: A, B, and D. It has not done that. The financing of Medicare is a big blur. Since parts B and D were added: the costs have not been totally paid for by enrollees—and those costs have been added to the National Debt.

When, Medicare Part D, prescription coverage for seniors, was added in 2006: it added $47.4 billion to the National Debt.

To solve the future deficit problem: all of Medicare costs must be paid by the Medicare payroll tax, premiums, and tax revenues. If, any part is paid for by borrowing—you are passing that debt to future generations. That is wrong. That is what the US congress and Obama is doing: the reduction in Medicare's deficit spending—is increased by the same amount to fund Obamacare. His new Medicare payroll tax is for part A. That is not the problem. It is part: B and D: part A has a surplus. The federal debt is accumulating and growing every year until the US government goes bankrupt—or it is rectified. We have not fixed Medicare's deficit spending, completely, and we are embarking on a new healthcare program that is costly—not correctly designed and not fully funded by new taxes and will add to the National Debt.

Reducing fraud and waste in Medicare, cutting benefits, eliminating non-essential drugs, changing the terms, and fully funding parts: B and D should have come first—in a separate bill before starting a new program.

Providing healthcare for the 31 million uninsured should have in a second, separate bill and fully funded by new taxes. Funding Obamacare up to two-thirds by transferring Medicare's deficit funding to Obamacare—perpetuates the red ink.

One reason—our healthcare cost per capital is higher than any country in the world: 66 percent of adults over 20 years are overweight and obese.

Congress has failed to act responsibly: **HR 3950—Patients Protection and Affordable Act**—has, at least, 15 missing elements:

1. The public option [i.e., government provided healthcare paid-for by taxes].

2. The soda-junk food tax: that would accomplish two things: help reduce obesity and pay for medical costs.
3. Higher co-pays and deductibles for people who's BMI exceed certain levels or 25% or more of body weight.
4. The trans-fat ban in processed food: known to cause plaque buildup in the arteries.
5. Tort reform
6. It did not properly fund Obamacare.
7. End-of-life counseling
8. The right to die...
9. Did not include caps...
10. The Dr. Kevorkian option
11. It protects the patient from the abusive insurer—it does not protect the insurer from the abusive patient.
12. It did not achieve universal healthcare.
13. **HR 3950**—does allow 50% higher premiums for smokers:—but, it turned a blinded eye to homosexuals—or gays: their medical expenses are much higher than straights—due to higher rates of STD (syphilis, HIV/AIDS, gonorrhea, HPV infections, hepatitis A and B, herpes, the "gay" bowel disease, etc.)—and other related medical costs. Here are the hard, cold facts:
    a. the rate of new HIV cases—44 times higher for gays
    b. MSM accounted for 71% of all HIV infections—in 2005
    c. smokers rate 3 times higher
    d. alcohol use 7 times higher
    e. 17 times more likely to develop anal cancer
    f. illicit drug use 19 times higher

A study by the Family Research Institute found:

— Smokers cost US taxpayers $156 billion a year—or little over $3,000 per person.
— Homosexuals cost US taxpayers $102 billion a year—or more than $25,000 person.

Conclusion: I don't believe it is fair to force straights to pay the medical cost of homosexuals or gays: they need to form a non-profit medical group to treat this group—or, like the case for smokers, allow medical providers to raise premiums to pay the full medical cost of this group by this group. It is something they choose to do. I think, when Lot's wife—in Genesis 19—looked back at Sodom and Gomorrah being destroyed by fire and turned into a pillar of salt—it symbolizes: she became wise, by looking at consequences of homosexual behavior—or these statistics.

14. HR 3590 lacks fairness: straights are not responsible for the STDs of homosexuals.
15. Obama did not tell truth of cost.

One must realize, the $849 billion estimated cost for the first ten years is for six years of benefits—enrollment in the insurance plans offered through the government sponsored state exchanges—begins in 2014 and will gradually increase until the 31 million are covered. The next decade—the cost will explode, when fully implemented.

You can not fund Obamacare in the next decade—by reducing $500 billion in fraud, waste and inefficiency—because, it would have already been eliminated. It must come from new taxes or it will increase the deficit by that amount.

We are using misleading accounting principles—to delude the public, like Enron, that eventually led to its implosion. Maybe, that is what is necessary for the US government—to make changes.

The government, like some people—don't make life-style changes until they have a stroke—or are faced with death. They want premium healthcare without paying for it. That is not going to work.

I don't trust the US government without surveillance—or a look at the books. The fast growing $13.4 trillion National Debt is proof—it has not done a good job. It has not made all the figures public. For one thing: it does not explain the gap in the budget deficit—and the increase in the annual National Debt.

Nor, do we know what the real Medicare deficit is for the next ten years for parts B and D—or the total cost of Obamacare. The Obama $849 billion health reform bill is a mixture of Medicare, the CLASS Act, SCHIP, Medicaid and Obamacare finances and it does not include all state costs. It is a big blur: the breakdown.

I read in the LA Times: $500 billion will be paid in tax subsidies to low and moderate income individuals and families to help buy insurance over the next ten years—it did not give the cost of tax credits to small employers. These two tax credits or subsidies—plus the cost of administrating it: plus the grants to states for expanding Medicaid are the major costs of the new healthcare plan.

The major new taxes to fund Obamacare (i.e, for the uninsured) total: $250.9 billion—most of the rest is a bogus transfer of money from Medicare cost reductions. The figures reported in the LA Times do not add up. There is a lot missing! And, there is no clear picture on the Internet that I can find. The CBO does not give one—either. That makes—Obama's plan difficult to analyze. The government should give a clear picture.

Yahoo News reported: 4/7/10: **Nearly half of US households escape federal income tax.** That number will increase, when you add the Obama healthcare tax credits. That is headed in the wrong direction. Curtis Dubay, senior tax analyst at the Heritage Foundation says: "We have 50 percent of people who are getting something for nothing."

Congressman Jim Clybum says he is "giddy" over the numbers....

I think the Congress and Obama are running the US government off a cliff; if, it does not do as David Walker says: impose a budget on how much the federal government spends on Medicare, change our payment systems, our tax incentives, our taxpayer subsidies.... These, he says, are absolutely essential.

I would add: the people should do more to "turn off the faucet of chronic disease" as Dr. Roizen says by doing four things and reduce medical costs, substantially, and the government should reform the tax code to generate enough revenue to pay government outlays and should give the American people an annual report, like corporations do for shareholders—in concise and simple terms.

Part I: Medicare: revenues and expenditures and the bottom line: surplus or deficit.

Part II: Obamacare (i.e., for the uninsured).

Medicare parts A, B, C, D, Medicaid, Social Security, SCHIP, CLASS, FEHBP, etc—should be treated like subsidiaries with separate financial statements—and then put together. So, we know where we stand and what to do next—in each program.

I believe, it would have been better to use the $500 billion in Medicare savings to reduce the federal debt.

Why add back $500 billion in deficit spending to fund Obamacare; why, not fully fund it. The congress did half-a-job.

The good thing: the bill provides healthcare insurance for the 31 million uninsured and contains some good parts. The bad thing: it is about one-third funded by new taxes and two-thirds funded by deficit spending. The $500 billion funding from savings in the present Health care system is full of holes.

It is a fallacy—to think—you can fund Obamacare perpetually (i.e., decade after decade)—by reducing $500 billion in waste and fraud in Medicare and Medicaid. He said, this waste and fraud was "currently" in our healthcare system; therefore, once, it is wiped out—you can use this means of financing in the next decade, etc.

The bill is called: Affordable [healthcare]—that is subject to proof: the consequences of all these costly provisions. The CEO of Aetna says: it will, likely, cause premiums to increase.

I call the Obama statement: it will reduce the deficit $138 billion in the next 10 years and $1.2 trillion in the next ten years: a misleading sales pitch—to win public approval.

I blame in part—the CBO.

I want to remind you: in 2001, the CBO projected budget surpluses would total $5.4 trillion in the next ten years beginning with 2002: it was just the opposite: deficits totaled: $6.49 trillion [including 2011 est.].

I think the Obama figures are prefabricated to promote optimism— and highly unreliable, particularly, the second decade.

The cost of Medicare was seven times the initial estimate—after 25 years. Obamacare will more likely, add $1.338 trillion to the deficit in the next 20 years—than reduce: based on HR 3590 funding.

Here is where Obamacare also falls short, he said: to the AMA his budget recently passed, would set aside a $635 billion Health Reserve Fund over ten years—over half the amount would came from limiting the tax deductions of wealthiest Americans. That is the 28 percent cap: rejected by congress—or Republicans.

He is short: an estimated $318 billion. He must pass another tax—or this will be added to the deficit.

Here is another defect: what if some influential senator said: I want to use the $500 billion saved in Medicare to build a US network of **bullet trains**—that would leave Obamacama 2/3rds unfunded.

Does Obama have first dibs on this money to fund his new healthcare plan for the uninsured? No.

Anyways, this is a shenanigan; because, the alleged $500 billion saved in Medicare means: it reduces the federal deficit $500 billion and leaves no surplus tax revenues or cash in the treasury to fund Obamacare. Don't you see—this is bullshit financing—the money does not exist.

Obama must increase taxes $500 billion—or he will create a new $500 billion federal deficit. The goal should be to stop deficit financing of all entitlement programs, such as: Medicare, Medicaid, and Obamacare.

He also told the AMA—he would save $25 billion—by preventing: readmissions to hospitals. He believes this savings will help pay for his healthcare plan. It doesn't. It stays in the Medicare Hospital Insurance Fund. His plan is funded by different taxes, fees, and fines that go into the US Treasury.

UPDATE

Twenty-six states have filed a lawsuit against the Obama health care reform law, saying: they can't afford it. George says: expanding Medicaid would cost $1.54 to $1.79 billion and insists the federal government pick of the total tab. So, Obama's estimated cost of $849 billion did not include total cost to states.

Employers are devising strategies to avoid the cost of enforcement; such as, replacing full time employees with part time.

Recent Republican report says: Obama's health care law will cost states $118.04 billion through 2023—double the CBO estimate.

Healthcare providers have announced increases of premiums as much as 59.3% in 2010. March 12, 2011 Blue Cross said hikes could reach 86.5%. More increases are likely in the future—as the plan is implemented.

March 18, 2011: CBO increased the estimated cost of the new healthcare law by about $90 billion, to $1.13 trillion, from 2012 to 2021.

After skimming through the 2074 page text of HR 3590—it is a monstrosity of new regulations—and I concluded: there must be a better way to do this. No Republican voted for it—for obvious reasons: the nation can't afford it right now and it has objectionable components.

Yet, we need sensible healthcare reform.

The good thing: the bugs can be worked out and parts restructured or even repealed—and replace with a better, simpler, and less costly national healthcare program. Time will tell what is bad.

Might that plan—be **The Healthy Americans Act**—Yea, but there is no way to know for sure, except by more study and testing.....

Posted 5/29/10

TWO SAGES, PART 1 [revised 6/15/20 & 7/21/10]

Bill Moyer, the Populist

In his final broadcast: he revealed his bias—or heart-felt beliefs: here it is. He said, "Plutocracy and democracy don't mix" and he defines plutocracy as: "the rule of the rich, political power by the wealthy"—and most importantly, he states: it has "become an American phenomenon."

Bias is not bad, if based on facts.

And he quotes a report by Citigroup with an "equity strategy" for their investors, entitled, "Revisiting Plutonomy: The Rich Getting Richer." Here are some excerpts:

"Asset booms, a rising profit share and favorable treatment by market-friendly governments have allowed the rich to prosper....[and] take an increasing share of income and wealth over the last 20 years..."

"...the top 10%, particularly the top 1% of the US—plutonomist in our parlance—have benefited disproportionately from the productivity boom, at the relative expense of labor."

"....[and they] are likely to get even wealthier in the coming years. [Because] the dynamics of plutonomy are still in tact."

Bill Moyers said Wall Street giant Citigroup—back in 2005 coined the word—plutonomy—a variation of plutocracy—as an economic system were the privileged few make sure the rich get richer with the government on their side.

You know—I have said that for years, but despite getting the greater share of total income; particularly, the top 1%: their taxes have been reduced by Reagan and Bush—and the US national debt has gone from billions to trillions. Both his and my message has been suppressed or not been made public by the Mass Media.

I have never seen Bill Moyers—on Face the Nation, Meet the Press, This Week, or on the McLaughlin Group, Washington Week, he surely is not a regular guest on Fox News Sunday, etc.

Here is more proof—my book, *The Estate Tax and Politics,* has sold only one copy since publication in 2006. Plutocrats hate the estate (or inheritance) tax: it threatens their existence.

My book, *Why the Reagan and Bush Tax-cuts are Unfair* (second edition), has sold only a few copies: total royalties [all books]: $41.08.

My book, *The Tax Guardian.Com*—postings from my blog from 1/22/08 to 1/31/09, has sold no copies, since publication in July 2009—despite my effort to inform the public on my Blog, letters to particular persons, and a 1 million email marketing campaign.

Compare this to Sarah Palin's book—*Going Rogue,* which sold 700,000 copies the first week. The difference: mass media backing (not intrinsic value). Mine has greater intrinsic value: that is my bias.

The plutonomy owes and controls the mass media—there has been a [near] 100 percent blockage of my message. No reviews. I have given my books to major TV news casters, magazine journalists, and sent a letter to over a hundred newspaper editors informing them of my tax book and blog: charging the Bush Administration of budget deficit deception and criticized the Reagan and Bush tax cuts, favoring the rich, nothing has been made public. Of the four billionaires that I sent a letter: Warren Buffett, Ross Perot, Peter G. Peterson, Michael Bloomberg: none have answered. They love the Reagan and Bush tax cuts. They believe—they individually deserved 85% of the unearned income and the nation 15%: I don't.

☺ Even, ex-VP Al Gore is afraid to open his mouth, who now sits on the board of several large corporations.

☺ William H. Gates Sr. is the co-author with Chuck Collins of "Wealth and our Commonwealth: Why America should tax Accumulated Fortunes"—both of whom I sent my book: "The Estate Tax and Politics"—complementing theirs—I have heard from neither one.

I question whether these millionaires and billionaires want fair tax reform; if, they did, they would say or do something: to bring these truths to the public attention. They have not. My question:

Do you agree or disagree? Put it into record and put your money behind tax reform: enlightening the public. Warren Buffett—says: he going to give 50% of his money away: I have not received a dime.

Bill Moyers says, "In this regard (i.e., frankness, sincere, open, free, clear, and without deceit), I take my cue from the late Edward R. Murrow, the Moses of broadcast news."

Like Murrow, Bill Moyers is shunned by the mass media for his bias—and therefore, his journal is on the Public Broadcasting System.

He says, according to study from the Pew Research Center last month, nine out of ten Americans give our economy a negative rating. Eight out of ten report difficulty finding jobs in their communities, and seven out of ten say they experienced job related or financial problems over the last year.

That is not true of Goldman Sachs: it dispersed $5.4 billion in executive bonuses: the first three months of this year. That is obscene.

UPDATE

Lloyd Blankein, the CEO of GS, received $14.12 million in compensation for 2010, including a cash bonus of $4.5 million, $7.65 million in stock grants, and perks worth $404,067—$185,000 car and driver, $63,020 medical and dental coverage, and $18,695 in life insurance premiums, etc.

These three perks are tax-free.

In addition, he was given restricted stock valued a t $12.6 million, up from $9 million in 2009, which is not counted in total annual compensation.

This income is not taxed until vested.

It does not stop there: he received $27.2 million from his investment in private funds managed by Goldman Sachs.

Long-term capital gains and dividends are taxed at a low 15%, thanks to our US congressmen.

This shows—how low paid people do most of the work—and the top 1 percent, reap a disproportional share of the nation's income.

Thanks to President Bush—the limits on itemized deductions for high incomers in 2010—are 100% removed.

Now, the question is: how much did he pay in taxes—after all tax deductions, tax breaks, and tax loopholes are utilized?

That is the dark side of the picture.

Moyer concluded: "So, it is that like those populist of that earlier era, millions of Americans have awakened to a sobering reality; they live in a plutocracy, where they are disposable. Then, the remedy was a populist insurgency that ignited the spark of democracy.

Now, we have come to another parting of ways, and once again the fate and character of our country are up for grabs."

Warren Buffett, the Plutonomist

In his company's last annual meeting: Buffett and Munger snacked on peanut brittle and fudge from See's Candies, a Berkshire unit. Despite the nutritionists claim: sugar is your enemy. He is also a big investor in Coca-Cola. Soda drinks, I believe, are a major cause of the US diabetes epidemic. People cannot resist the taste and feel good sugar high it gives.

Plutocrats don't care....what is important to them profits. Buffett has been accused of saying, "I'll tell you why I like the cigarette business. It cost a penny to make. Sell it for a dollar. It's addictive. And there's fantastic brand loyalty."

Here is Buffett's bias: he defended Goldman Sachs, saying: "I do not hold against Goldman the fact that an allegation has been made by the U.S. Securities and Exchange Commission."

His vice chairman is more explicit: he told shareholders, "he would have voted against SEC prosecution."

Their bias is not based on facts.

They are bias, because Buffett has a $5 billion investment in the company; notwithstanding, Matt Baibbi of the Rolling Stones states: Goldman Sachs is a "great vampire squid wrapped around the face of humanity, relentlessly, jamming its blood funnel into anything that smells like money." Buffett defends: Abacus 2007 AC1—marketing to investors—[shitty] RMBS—designed to fail.

What is important to Buffett, as he said: "Our (GS) preferred are paying $15 every second, so as we sit here, 'tick, tick, tick, tick," that's $15 every second....and that well go on, and we'll be getting $500 million a year....We love the investment."

However, there is another side to the coin: the losers—or victims of Wall Street's fraudulent schemes: investors, shareholders, and taxpayers. They have a different viewpoint. They say, "Crooks and thieves, lock em' up."

Here is another thing: in 2008, Goldman Sachs paid $14 million in taxes (i.e., 1% of net profit) and paid $4.8 billion in executive bonuses (i.e., more than double the company's net profit): shareholders have filed a lawsuit. This shows how corrupt and lopsided the US tax code is and our system of compensation. Blankfein, the CEO, received a salary and bonus package of $68.5 million in 2007.

Warren Buffett says on replacing Lloyd Blankfein, "If Lloyd had a twin brother, I would vote for him."

I guess, he sees nothing wrong with GS & Co and Fabrice Tourre, a GS-VP, defrauding investors and violating sections of the Security Exchange Act. Those are some of the SEC charges. At the center of this complaint: is a synthetic collateralized debt obligation or CDO tied to reams of residential mortgages—named Abacus 2007 AC1. Buffett analysis of the case is faulty and partial. He said, "I have no problem with that Abacus transaction." He thinks it was two sides betting against the other. He left out the fact, it was rigged. Let me explain for the public:

John Paulson, the shark, looking to make a killing (i.e., financial) with a big pile of chips: comes to Goldman Sachs—saying: he wants to take a short position on reams of triple B—RMBS [residential mortgage backed securities]; primarily, originated in the second half of 2006.

Goldman Sachs acted as the facilitator and put Fabrice Tourre in charge of structuring and marketing.

To do this—Goldman Sachs set up a special purpose vehicle or SPV in the Cayman Islands—called Abacus 2007 AC1, because, it was finalized in April 2007, and AC1, because GS created a number of abacuses.

Because, this was a synthetic CDO—there was no underlying assets in Abacus AC1—they were based on the ABX (i.e., the triple B mortgage price index)—that calculates the changing value of the mortgage backed bonds. The reference portfolio of Abacus was based on RMB bonds—in the ABX. Certain ones were selected and structured into classes or tranches—in Abacus. Long investors would bet—the value of these bonds would go up, if people paid their mortgage and house prices went up, and short investors would bet—the value of these bonds would go down, if people failed to pay their mortgages and house prices went down. This is capitalism gone amuck—nothing useful to mankind is produced by these investments—or bets. It diverts capital from the real economy—to Wall Street's casino gambling. Of course, Golden Sachs was the dealer—or bookie—and took a cut. To sell the synthetic RMB bonds: it was necessary to have someone that was competent in analyzing the credit risk of residential mortgages—to pick the portfolio of RMBS—for abacus, so, that it would not be weighted on one side—or appeal to long investors.

So, Goldman Sachs chose ACA Management LLC, an independent collateral manager, to pick the portfolio of residential mortgages in abacus, a synthetic $2 billion CDO—or collateralized debt obligation. The pitch book states: ACA, the "Portfolio Selection Agent"—and devoted 28 pages describing its experience, tract record, capabilities, staff, etc. Their stated investment philosophy: "preserve capital." This was important to long investors. Here is where the selection process went wrong. ACA was told by GS and Tourre, that Paulson was going to be a $200 million equity (or long) investor in the bonds, thinking he was a friend, aligned with their interests, they opened the door, and allowed him to help pick the collateral—or mortgages behind the bonds. His interest was contrary to ACA, a potential (long) investor and a unit if ACA Financial Guaranty Corp, bond insurer. Being a short investor, Paulson would pick the mortgages most likely to default.

He wanted to short triple B-RMBS originated in the second half of 2006. Why, because they would have little or no paid in equity—houses would have been purchased near the top of the market—not the bottom. According to the SEC complaint: Mr. Paulson, especially, wanted to find risky subprime adjustable-rate mortgages that had been given to borrows with low credit scores who lived in California, Arizona, Florida, and Nevada—states with big spikes in home prices that he reckoned would crash.

On this subject: there was communication between ACA and GS seeking clarification of Paulson's position: they did not get it. A written March 2007 memo—one month before Abacus closed—shows: ACA believed Paulson was in equity (long) investor. Failure of GS—to disabuse ACA of this misunderstanding is fraudulent behavior. The reason it did not: it would have nixed the deal.

All residential mortgages are not the same: the originator, the region, the price, the date, the type of mortgage, owner equity, FICO score, income, etc.—are important to determine risk. It was not proper for Paulson, who was secretly planning to short the RMBS—to select the mortgage portfolio—and he did 55 out of 90 reams—according to the allegations. This is like—looking at the cards and stacking the deck—before betting starts. I can't imagine, why ACA would allow Paulson, an outsider, to so this, if, they knew he was a short investor. It would have been insane for a unit of a bond insurer, to let some one to pick collateral, who hand an opposite interest to their own. This also important to equity investors—to know that the Abacus bonds did not favor CDS (short) investors over CDO (long) investors.

All the reams of residential mortgages in the abacus synthesized CDO were rated Baa—lowest investment grade—to start. These lowest investment grade mortgages were transformed by a process called: securitization by GS's SPV—into seven tranches: two rated triple A, highest grade investment bonds—by Moody's and S&P. It was bogus—two grades higher than they should have been. They should have been rated triple C or D—based on their performance, and the fact, the subordinate trances: B, C, D, and FL were never funded. Mortgage defaults are suppose to wipe out lower tranches before the higher. These two higher tranches rated triple A—were really—triple C—or junk bonds. Trust here is important—because, investors do not; generally, examine the reference portfolio, in this case, 90 bonds backed by thousands residential mortgages. They depend on rating agencies. It this case, they failed to protect investors—to help GS sell the bonds for a fee.

This was not the spring and summer of the housing boom: it was the fall—prices peaked in mid 2006—and insiders knew the housing market collapse was eminent; not so much—foreign investors.

Here is the proof:

- Tourre knew this by this email sent to a friend, January 2007: "the whole building is about to collapse anytime now."
- Similarly—the head of the division in an email to Tourre said, "the CDO biz is dead and we don't have a lot of time left."

How did they know this:

A. The ABX (i.e., price index of RMBS)—fell sharply in February 2007, and slightly recovered in March.
B. House prices peaked in mid 2006 and begin a steady decline up to 2007 and beyond.
C. Mortgage delinquencies begin to rise in 2006 and rose sharply in 2007 and beyond—as well as—foreclosures.
D. Real GDP growth—contracted after 2005.
E. Industry experts tract these number, because Goldman Sachs's—short positions increased, sharply, during 2007, meaning: they were betting the housing market would crash.

Back to Abacus AC1—the top or super senior tranche of the $2 billion synthetic CDO was unfunded—i.e., no one bought the bonds. Here is what happened. On these, Paulson took a short position—i.e., bet the mortgage backed bonds would default and lose value. Therefore, he insured them, by entering into a CDS, using Goldman Sachs as an intermediary, with ACA Capital through its subsidiary, ACA Financial Guaranty Corp, backed by ABN Amro, Dutch bank, which was acquired by the Royal Bank of Scotland, and when the bonds defaulted, ACA could not pay off, so the RBS had to pay Paulson: $840 million. And guess what: Paulson did not buy or own the bonds. This is a synthetic CDS or credit default swap, that pays him, if the bonds default, as if he owned them—but, did not. This sounds crazy, but the US congress made it legal. And, this is done OTC—with little oversight or regulation.

Of the seven abacus tranches: only the class A-1 and class A-2 bonds were sold, rated triple A. The rest of the CDO was unfunded. They failed to attract investors; but, they found one: IKB—a German bank.

Tourre knew IKB was interested in the triple A class—or so-called mezzanine bonds. It is higher than mid. It was triple A—highest investment grade. But, all the RMBS in the Abacus were triple B—lowest investment grade. The triple B—rated RMBS that Paulson was betting on were the same triple A rated RMBS—packaged in Abacus—that was marketed to long investors. How did they get upgraded? This process is called securitization or stacking them in order of subordination—or tranches; except, there were none. The class A-2 was first in line to be wiped out by defaults. The second step: pay rating agencies: to re-rate Baa RMB—triple A. There is no way in the world that these mid-and-subprime mortgages were triple A, highest investment grade—equal to municipal bonds or corporate 500 bonds. That is fraudulent.

The so-called triple A—mezzanine bonds, were not low risk, they were not ground floor: medium risk: they were basement floor: high risk.

Fabrice Tourre, who was in charge of structuring the abacus CDO tied to residential mortgages—is also in charge of marketing it. He knew the housing market was about to collapse—and had to act quickly. He was responsible for printing and sending out the 66 page pitch book—to potential investors. It mentioned: ACA was the largest investor, it was not—and stated ACA was the mortgage portfolio selector and omitted: Paulson helped pick fifty percent or more of the RMBS structured in Abacus—and planned on shorting them. Not knowing this—IKB invested $150 million in the two tranches.

ACA Capital bought $42 million of the class A-2 bonds—to show good faith. These are the only two (long) investors.

On these two tranches of bonds—Paulson also bought protection or a CDS, which pays him—if, they defaulted, and if you can believe this—on bonds he did not own, but owned by someone else, from Goldman Sachs, which laid off—the risk to a third party—Abacus SPV Ltd., an entity, registered in the Cayman Islands, for nefarious reasons. In this big stakes game: losers are legally bond to pay winner. Of course, GS was the dealer or seller. These two tranches of triple A rated mid-and-subprime mortgage bonds—promised to pay 85 basic points and 110 basic points higher than the LIBOR—that Paulson shorted; suffered a credit event; shortly, after being sold—and became toxic waste.

IKB, the German bank, who invested $150 million, and ACA, who invested $42 million—or bought the bonds: lost $192 million and Paulson made $192 million: that totals about $1 billion profit—on the residential mortgage backed $2 billion synthetic CDO—Abacus deal.

IKB and ABN, the two foreign banks, which lost a billion dollars, have filed a lawsuit. Buffett says, "The bank made a dumb deal." The SEC says the Abacus 2007 AC1 deal: defrauded investors. I agree.

Blankfein said at the Senate Hearing: "We certainly did not bet against our client." That was refuted by Senator Levin, who cited Timberwolf 1, which sold $600 million of these subprime mortgage backed securities—in early 2007—which the head of the division—called "one shitty deal." That is a different kind of CDO—than Abacus. These RMBS are from GS's own inventory—they wanted to dump on investors. The GS email to its sales force said: [selling] Timberwolf was a "top priority." It lost 80% of its value in 5 months. The story does not end here: Goldman shorted the same securities with AIG. That is betting against the securities that you are selling. That may not be illegal, but it is unethical.

Munger said on replacing Blankfein, "There are plenty of CEOs I'd like to see gone," but Blankfein is not one of them.

Apparently, they did not listen to his answer to Carl Levin's question at the Senate hearing—about the SEC complaint: he is a snake.

Matt Baibbi, who also called Goldman Sachs the "Great American Bubble Machine"—said: "[it] sits upon a Ponzi pyramid, preventing light to shine within its funnel." Can you see why Wall Streets hates the light? They want their shenanigans kept secret. Matt Baibbi says: Golden Sachs uses America [and the world] for its "pump and dump" scams. It is a giant investment bank—broker—market marker—hedge fund:

- Accused of lowering their quality standards and underwriting crappy IPOs during the dot-com bubble for a quick profit.
- Accused of a two-tier investment system: one for insiders and one for the public.
- Accused of market rigging
- Accused of dark pool trading
- Accused of securitizing and marketing crappy mortgage backed securities rated triple A during the housing boom and betting against them.
- Accused manipulating commodity prices.
- Accused of insider trading
- Accused of moral bankruptcy
- Fined for trading ahead of its clients
- Accused of using off-shore corporations to dodge taxes
- Fined for spinning and laddering: considered small—compared to gains.
- Fined for violating a naked short ban
- Accused of rigging the bailout
- Accused of using bailout money to pay executives extravagant bonuses
- Accused of HFT front running
- Accused of rigging tax vote
- Accused on unbridled greed
- Accused of managing banks in Bermuda and the Cayman Islands, where clients have secret accounts—used to avoid taxes
- Accused of co-opting the Federal Reserve and the US Treasury Department

- It has been hit with six recent lawsuits—alleging: breach of fiduciary duty, corporate waste, abuse of power, mismanagement, and unjust enrichment.
- The US Justice Department has opening a criminal investigation.

And the Congress; particularly, the Senate balks at stopping Wall Street's nefarious casino operations. Forty-four percent are millionaires. Many plan, when they leave office, to work for Wall Street firms for big money.

Congress is the stepping stone.

The plutonomy rules by making tons of money, paying low taxes on their unearned income, getting their men or alumni placed in key government jobs, hiring top government officials after leaving office in the Wall Street firms, by making political contributions,* by influential well-connected lobbyists, and by owning the mass media—enabling them to shut out the critical (or negative) light and influence voters or the public.

*Note: no Republican commissioner voted for the SEC prosecution. Some Republicans claim it is politically motivated—I find politically motivated. In March alone, Goldman Sachs donated $167,500 to Republican candidates and political entities; that is, one month before the SEC decision.

On the evening news: CBS's Katie Curic asked Anthony Mason, which side got the best of it at the Senate hearing: he said, it was about even: no it wasn't. The SEC case was strong: the executives deceitful.

Fabrice Tourre, the only man charged, says the charges are "false." No, they are not. Senator Levin presented indisputable evidence.

The executives claim: no wrong-doing.

But, here is were the SEC—fell short: they charged Fabrice Tourre, a Goldman Sachs VP, with defrauding investors, but not John Paulson, the other half of the scam or plot. He helped select the mortgages in the Abacus deal, which he intended to short, which is cheating. He made a billion dollars on his bet. Tourre got paid $2 million fee and Paulson paid Goldman Sachs $15 million fee—as the facilitator—and upper GS management approved the deal—so, it is culpable. Ninety-nine percent of these bonds were down graded in nine months and became nearly worthless. This is far more serious than the Martha Steward case. Tourre calls himself—the fabulous Fab—is a crook, thief, and liar. That is three strikes. My verdict, if the SEC charges are true: jail time for Paulson, the instigator and abettor, and Tourre, the forger and seller, and for him: a $4 million fine—and investor restitution paid by Paulson and a $200 million fine paid by Goldman Sachs and Paulson's Hedge Fund: half going to SEC and half going to the Justice Department, so, taxpayers don't get stuck with paying for these investigations and prosecutions. And, the third guilty party, which is not included in the SEC complaint: based on the facts I have seen: the two rating agencies, who miss-rated the abacus bonds: two grades—a fine: double the fee paid.

On ABC news: The Case Against Goldman Sachs: George Stephanopoulos had two guests: Suzy Welch and Jon Hilsenroth: both were bias for Goldman; rather than, having one critical—like Matt Baibbi or Max Keiser.

UPDATE

Goldman Sachs pays $550 million fine to settled charges that it defrauded investors: $250 million will be returned to investors and $300 million will be paid to the US Treasury.

You would not see Matt Baibbi—who called Golden Sachs "a giant vampire squid" interviewed on Meet the Press, or Face the Nation, or News Week—or Max Keiser. But, the mass media loves Warren Buffett—every major media outlet reported his support for Goldman Sachs. The reason: there is a lot support for Goldman Sachs: there are a lot of big institutions invested. The giant investment bank-hedge fund, changed into a holding company—so, it could qualify for TARP bailout money and borrow money from the Federal Reserve at low interest rates. That is another scam: being a hedge fund—it does not qualify. However, the big media does not pick up, everything Buffet says. They filter out what they don't like, for example:

Do you know, Warren Buffett has said: the estate [or inheritance] tax protects the US from becoming a plutocracy; notwithstanding, President

Bush done his best to repeal it—permanently. He also tried to eliminate the tax on dividends, but failed. But, succeeded in lowering the tax on dividends and capital gains to 15 percent: two big sources of income of the wealthy. He is an un-American freakin plutonomist. But, is Buffett a hypocrite? Berkshire Hathaway has developed and markets life insurance polices that help people avoid state and federal estate taxes.

I sent Buffett a copy of my book, *The Estate Tax and Politics,* in May of 2007, which explains why the estate tax should not be repealed—a goal of the Republican Party—and asked him, "Whether, you think the American people—deserve to read this book?" He did not answer.

By the way, his vice chairman, Charlie Munger, is a Republican, Buffett's alter-ego. Buffett is a fake literal.

He stated the US tax code is unfair: stating he paid 19% of his income for 2006 of $48.1 million in total federal taxes—where as, his employees, who made far less: paid 33 percent, but he does not put his money behind tax reform. He is currently, the world's third richest man—and pays very little taxes.

I wrote Buffett a second letter in 2008, asking to comment on an article I wrote on my blog—entitled: "The Oracle of Omaha", which he also failed to answer. I don't think he wants to change the tax code.

So, I sent him this third letter and a backup email to his corporate address: dated 5/29/10.

Dear Mr. Warren Buffett,

Twice—I wrote to you before and twice you failed to answer. This is the third time. I wrote an article about you on my blog: thetaxguardian. com—posted 5/29/10—entitled: The Two Oracles (or Sages), which I want you to read. The US House of Representatives Finance Service Committee called Goldman Sachs—"corrupt "—and you sided with them. You have committed a great moral transgression—or error—by defending Abacus 2007 AC1, that defrauded investors. However, you can absolve yourself—by sponsoring my website—or making a donation; so, that I can break through the big media blockage—and enlighten the world. You have no defense, lawyers can't help you, this is a moral issue—not legal. Playing the ukulele and singing won't help you—either. Only, one thing can help you: penitence. What is your answer? I have a contact page at the end of my blog. Don't deny me for the third time. It is not alright to sell a box of See's Chocolates, made with low grade synthetic ingredients, rather than high grade natural—to make a bigger profit, and not tell you trusting customers—or Goldman Sachs to sell asset backed securities that it misrepresents or bets against. If, you do—there is something wrong with your moral compass. You need to read what Jesus said about the rich man.

The U.S. and world tax guardian,

Walter Franklin Picca

When and if he answers: I will post it on my blog. This will show how much he loves America!

I have received no answer—as of July 1, 2011.

Posted 6/24/10

TWO SAGES, PART II [corrected 7/23/10]

The Financial Crisis Inquiry Commission investigating the rating agencies that gave top triple A ratings to mortgage backed securities that subsequently plunged in value—subpoenaed **Warren Buffett, the Plutonomist,** to testify. However, like defending Goldman Sachs—Mr. Buffett also defended the rating firms. Why, because, his company is one of the biggest shareholders of Moody's Investor Service—and sat right next to the CEO at the hearing. Here is what he said, "They made a mistake that virtually everyone in the country made." That answer is bias and incorrect.

Ellen Seidman, former director of the Treasury's Office of Thrift Supervision, said in February 2000, "Subprime lending, which involves lending to borrowers who have a significant higher risk of default based on their credit repayment history, has been the subject of intensive higher OTS scrutiny by our policy and supervisory staff for several years. We started sounding warnings about risks arising from this lending activity as early as June 1998."

In 2000, Edward Gramlich, a Federal Reserve Governor, urged Alan Greenspan to crack down on subprime mortgage lenders. He said, "These practices....can result in consumers losing much of their equity in their home, or even the home itself." He says, Greenspan was opposed to it.

Jodie Bernstein, Director of the Bureau of Consumer Protection [1995-2001], said, "This is outrageous, that they're bundling these things up and then nobody has any responsibility for them. They're just passing them on."

Back in August 2004, Dean Baker, an economist, in an article in the Nation—entitled: "The Bush House of Cards" warned: that a housing bubble was forming, that it was political being ignored, and said:[when it happens] "the crash of the housing market will not be pretty."

Back in May 2006, Michael Hudson, an economist, predicted the "coming real estate collapse" in an article in Harper's Magazine—entitled: "The New Road to Serfdom" meaning debt. According to his chart, 90 percent of the growth of debt from 2000 to 2005 was real estate mortgages.

Another of his charts: shows house prices quadrupled from 1995 to 2004, while, national income remained about the same: that is a growing housing bubble without sustenance. People were lured into buying homes with easy credit—they could not afford --or with insufficient income.

He said, "Nearly half the people buying their first home last year were allowed to do so with no money down, and many of them took out so-called interest-only loans, for which payment of the actual debt—amortization— was delayed by several years. A few even took on "negative amortization" loans, which dispense entirely with payments on the principal and require only partial payment of the interest itself."

He compared the real estate bubble in Japan a decade earlier to the US housing market, he said: "as the price went up, banks lent more money than people could afford to pay interest on. Eventually, no one could afford to buy any more land, and demand fell off, and prices dropped accordingly."

He said, "We have already reached our own peak." And quoted Alan Greenspan, who said: home price had "risen to unsustainable levels" in some places and would have exceeded the reach of many Americans—if it won't for interest only loans and adjustable rate mortgages. And he said, "If this trend continues, homeowners and banks alike could be exposed to significant losses."

Hudson predicted when home prices fall, home buyers would be caught in a negative equity trap—i.e., owing more than the house was worth. "They can't sell," he said, "Their only choice is to cut back spending in other areas or lose the house—and everything they paid for it—in foreclosure."

That is what happened. The Case-Shiller house price index, shows that housing prices peaked in mid-2006—and begin a steady decline—but, the sad thing: not the amount owed on mortgages.

Goldman Sachs was well aware of this: it began losing money on their inventory of subprime mortgages—in the first ten days of December of 2006—according to a Business Insider report by Henry Blodget—and on December 14th, Goldman's CFO David Viniar and other executives decided to reverse course and begin shorting the housing market.

John Paulson, founder of one of the largest hedge funds, foreseen the subprime mortgage meltdown—and also bet short.

He was not the only one.

How did they—know? They watch the numbers: house prices, delinquency and foreclosure rates, ABX mortgage index, sales, etc. The housing boom was over. Yet, Goldman Sachs continued to market these RMBS to the unwary investors—who were still asleep or impervious to the facts.

Raymond McDaniel, the CEO of Moody's, blame their stellar ratings of junk MB bonds—primarily on the unprecedented collapse of the housing prices.

That is a phony excuse: here is the real reason expressed by Mark Froeba, former senior vice president at Moody's, said: he and others had been pressured by higher-ups to assign high ratings to securities issued by investment banks.

These are his exact words, "They used intimidation to create a docile population of analysts afraid to upset investment bankers and ready to cooperate to the maximum extent possible."

Analysts could be fired—if, banks were dissatisfied with their ratings. At one point: 53% of Moody's revenues were from rating these structured financial securities. Mark Froeba said: integrity and quality of ratings were sacrificed to increase the firm's market share and revenues. To accomplish this: a professional team of analysts were transferred [or fired] and replaced with non-experts.

Erick Kolchinsky, another ex-Moody's official, testified: analysts were given "no time to conduct adequate reviews of the securities." They needed weeks, instead they were given days, they did not have the resources, they were intimidated to make favorable ratings, discouraged independent research, and were overworked and underpaid. He said the firm chose profits over quality ratings.

For example, Moody's rated two tranches of Abacus 2007 AC1—Aaa (safest investment grade). There was no justification for this, if you look at the credit applications or data behind these subprime mortgages: the house prices, type of mortgage, monthly payments, income, FICO score, and the vulnerability of these types of loans: to falling house prices, higher interest rates, economic downturn, job loss, etc. Common sense would tell you— these subprime mortgages—would likely become delinquent and end up in foreclosure in the next four years. The bonds in Abacus were 3.9 to 4.9 years: all written in the last 18 months (i.e., during the top of the housing market). There would be little or no home owner paid-in equity. Despite these facts, they were rated Aaa, safest investment, historical with a loss of .05 percent. That is fraud. There were no reasonable grounds for these ratings. Today, over half the mortgages in Abacus are in default or foreclosure.

The rating firm's method of evaluating risk—or computer program— was designed to rubber stamp structured financial products—highest investment grade. That is fraud, when you leave out relevant risk factors, such as: low FICO scores of home buyers, income to debt, debt to equity, late payments, falling house prices, rising interest rates, etc.

But, the investment banks were equally at fault.

They would employ a wide variety of techniques to get higher ratings— such as: applied improper influence on rating firms, rushed ratings, omitted relevant information, and hired their employees—to help structuring their investment products, so that the rating firm's method of evaluating risk or computer program, would give out the ratings they wanted. Carl M. Levin described the operation as: "A conveyor belt of high-risk securities, backed by toxic mortgages, got AAA rating that turned out not to be worth the paper they were printed on."

Triple A ratings were necessary to market these bonds to institutional investors that the law mandates: must be triple A. Rigging ratings: by investment banks and rating firms—individually or jointly is fraud.

Sylvian Raynes, a former Moody's VP, said: the company engaged in a "pattern of fraud." He was fired for raising concerns about ratings on several deals. And, he was yanked off the air on CNBC—for expressing his opinion. He accused Jim Cramer, a CNBC analyst of being a PR agent for Goldman Sachs, who I thought was clearly bias and out of order (or obnoxious).

This verifies what I have said.

Over 90 percent of the AAA rated RMBS issued in 2006 and 2007 have been down graded to junk status. Unforeseen circumstances was not the primary problem. "You will get sick reading through these documents"—wrote David Dayen, editor of the FDL News, "They show that the rating agencies knew about the imminent collapse of the housing market through fraud and subprime loans as far back as 2004." The real problem: the rating agencies collaborated with the investment banks to make a profit until they were no longer able to dupe investors.

Moody's CEO, Mark McDaniel's, defense: the subprime mortgage meltdown came without warning—like a dam that broke—is false.

On March 13, 2007, the Mortgage Bankers Association reported a spike in subprime delinquencies and foreclosures in the fourth quarter of 2006. Yet, rating agencies continued to rate these mortgage backed bonds: triple A.

Erick Kolchinsky, the MD of rating subprime CDOs, said, "By 2007, we were barely keeping up with the deal flow and the developments in the market." Investment banks wanted to unload their subprime mortgages backed securities on to investors in a hurry—and they wanted highest investment ratings—before investors were fully aware of what was happening.

Ben Bernnake—in May of 2007—at the 43rd Federal Reserve Bank of Chicago annual conference—warned of troubles in the subprime mortgage market; particularly, adjustable-rate mortgages.

Erich Kolchinsky testified, "During the course of that year, the group which rated and monitored subprime bonds did not react to the deterioration in their performance statistics."

Their business model was wrong—instead of doing risk analysis for the benefit of investors—they were making false ratings to please bankers, who wanted to dump their risky RMBS onto uninformed investors.

Kolchinsky was demoted and transferred to a different department, one month after telling senior managers, their method of ratings were behind the times. Eventually, he left or was fired.

So, Raymond McDaniel, Moody's CEO is a liar. These erroneous ratings were not human error: it was systematic and intentional—to increase market share and maximize company profits. Senior management bullied its analysts into making these bogus ratings that contributed to the housing bubble-burst. Their delayed rating downgrades—had the effect of a dam-break.

But, Warren Buffett had nothing to do with these ratings. The person that the commission should have subpoenaed is Fabrice Tourre, the co-facilitator of Abacus 2007 AC1. He sent an email to a friend—that he was having trouble persuading Moody's to give the deal the rating he desired.

He is a con man. Why, he expressed in an email January 23, 2007, the housing related CDO market was about to collapse—and at the same time—he was seeking a triple A, highest investment rating, from Moody's for the RMB bonds in Abacus. This is unethical behavior.

For this unethical behavior: Goldman Sachs—gave Tourre a $2 million bonus—as the co-facilitator of Abacus 2007 AC1. Goldman Sachs has two American flags in front of their headquarters in New York City—I don't believe this company should represent—the way America does business—making money by swindling investors.

The commission—should ask GS-VP-Tourre—who at Moody's was he communicating with, what did he say—how did he get these subprime mortgage backed bonds—rated triple A—and question the person at Moody's—who he was dealing with; if, you wanted to get to the bottom of this. Without the Aaa rating: the Abacus 2007 AC1 bonds would have failed to attract long investors.

So, rating agencies are a big part of this swindle. The entire housing industry was corrupt. It begin with the mortgage mills, like Countrywide, IndyMac, New Century Financial, Ameriquest Mortgage, and thousands of lending affiliates of banks and thrifts—churning out toxic subprime mortgages—or liar loans—along with the investment banks, that bought these pools of subprime mortgages—securitizing them into MBS—and paid rating agencies to rate them highest investment grade; so, they could market them to the dumb, deceived, and trusting investors. And the US congress: deserves part of the blame for the failure to regulate the housing industry and derivatives: the transformation of high risk debt into low risk assets—or so-called: SIVs or CDOs.

For these unfair, deceptive, and illegal business practices—to maximize profits—and gain a large share of the market revenues: that resulted in the loss of billions of dollars to institutional investors, such as: pension funds, college endowments, municipalities, insurance companies, etc.—Raymond McDaniel, CEO of Moody's was paid: $8.8 million in 2007. He belongs in jail with other Moody executives.

These phony ratings could have been avoided, if analysts and executives were penalized for making inaccurate ratings—and rewarded for making accurate. But, instead, they are rewarded, if they make bad ratings and increase the company's market share of credit rating revenues and profits.

If, that were the case, Moody's CEO would have lost over ninety percent of his compensation and that would be still too much. He is a snake.

Integrity and accurate ratings could have diminished the size of the subprime mortgage bubble and burst, in which investors, home buyers, and shareholders lost trillions.

I would like to warn the Nation—the New Road to Serfdom—is the rising National Debt—as of June 24, 2010: $13.1 trillion. The interest on the National Debt to June 1: $248 billion. That is the next ticking time bomb.

The basic cause: high spending and low taxation—and gridlock in the Congress: the Senate neutralizing the House.

Related to this problem: one of Michael Hudson's chart shows: that the top 1% received a rising share of the nation's income; i.e., from interest, dividends and capital gains, and the bottom 80 percent—a decreasing share from 1979 to 2003. At the end of 2003: the top 1 percent received about four times the amount of the bottom 80 percent. Another chart shows: that capital gains tax was reduced from 39 percent in 1976--down to the current 15 percent. Besides that: Bush lowered the tax on dividends and income. So, the national debt is going up, the rich are getting richer, and the bottom 80 percent losing ground—and the Senate, primarily, blocks not only meaningful financial reform, but higher taxes on rich—who have received an increasing share of the wealth. That is not right.

Bill Moyers, the Populist, is right: plutocracy or plutonomy has become an American phenomenon. Why is this? He asked—and gives this answer: "Because over the past 30 years the plutocrats or plutonomists—choose your poison—have used their vastly increased wealth to capture the flag and assure the government does their bidding." That in part, is the Reagan and Bush tax cuts, highly favoring the rich. That may be changing—since Obama's election.

The congress is now working on financial reform—but, critics say, there are loopholes.

There is no justification for synthetic CDO and CDS.

Banks insured by the FDIC—should not be allowed to do proprietary trading; but, will the Volcher rule be enacted. The Merkley-Levin amendment is a version of the Volcher rule—and here is something that should be noted: of the 24 co-sponsors: not one is a Republican.

I agree with Charlie Munger, the VP of Berkshire Hathaway: "What we need is a new version of Glass-Steagall." Conglomerates of commercial and investment banks, brokerage companies, hedge funds, and insurance companies—should be broken up—for numerous reasons.

Reuters reported April 13, 2010,—U.S. Senate Republican leaders say: "no" on bank reform bill.

A tax on financial transactions is fair to pay for policing the industry—and protecting investors from fraud. But, it has no traction in congress.

Here is another prime example—of how the government does the bidding for the US plutocracy.

HR 1728, the Mortgage Reform and Anti-Predatory Lending Act of 2009, was passed May 9, 2009, by the House: 300-114. It is stalled in the Senate. Rep. Brad Miller, author of the legislation, says: Republicans argue: "now—is not the right time" to pass the bill.

It was not the right time in 2007: HR 3915, the Mortgage Reform and Anti-Predatory Lending Act of 2007, was passed by the House 291-123. President Bush threatened to veto it. It never made it through the Senate.

It was not the right time in 2005: HR 1182, the Prohibit Predatory Act, sponsored by Rep. Brad Miller with 66 Democrat and 1 Independent co-sponsors: never came up for a vote in the congress controlled by Republicans.

It was not the right time in 2002: Senator Sarbanes introduced a bill to curb abusive lending practices: no Republican was a co-sponsor. It died in committee. It is easier to kill bills in the Senate: fewer members.

It was not the right time in 2000: Rep. LaFalce introduced a bill—to curb abusive predatory lending practices and correct gaps in HOEPA. The bill would also have barred lenders from making loans without regard for the borrower's ability to repay the debt. Kat Aaron, in an article for the Center for Public Integrity, wrote: "A coalition of subprime lenders sprang into action to fight LaFalce's bill and other attempts to impose restrictions."

Predatory lending involves: equity stripping, abusive loan terms, high interest rates, loan flipping, prepayment penalties, yield spread premiums, inflated appraisal, excessive fees, falsifying information, and other unscrupulous practices.

In 2001, Irv Ackelsberg, an attorney with Community Legal Services, said at a hearing of the Senate Banking Committee, "I believe that predatory lending is the housing finance equivalent of the crack cocaine crisis. It is poison sucking the life out of our communities. And it is hard to fight because people are making so much money."

Did the Senate do anything? No.

Why? Since 1998, the financial industry spent over $3.9 billion lobbying members of congress.

Thirdly, Obama's tax proposals to end off-shore tax havens, loopholes, and tax breaks for corporations are also stalled in congress. That means: plutocrats continue to control congress. The war in Iraq and Afghanistan are 7 and 8 years old—and no tax has been enacted to pay for them. This is big cause of federal deficits—not Social Security, education, and healthcare.

Every major Reagan and Bush tax cut, except the 10% income tax bracket, constitutes legalized stealing. Congress refuses to pay for what they spend—that results in budget deficits.

Since Reagan—the top 20 percent of estates—owe back taxes—and the best way to collect that money is through the Death-Estate Tax. Taxing those who created the debt is more right, than future generations, who did not. In the last 30 years: $12 trillion has been added to the national debt.

The top marginal tax rates—eliminated by Reagan—should be restored: to reduce federal budget deficits. The long-term capital gains tax needs to be raised—and dividends subject to the income tax tables.

There are too many tax deductions and exemptions in the tax code—that makes it possible for individuals and corporations to reduce their taxes to zero. Let me give you one example, the McCourts—owners of the LA Dodgers—made $108 million from 2004 to 2009 and paid no state and federal income taxes.

Right now, there are a lot of crazy people running for office, including one—who wants to do away with Social Security and repeal the income tax, just won the Republican primary in Nevada: that is scary: people should be angry—but not crazy: others—want to lower or repeal their state income tax, like billionaire Meg Whitman in California. On tax issues, Steve Poizner was more right—but lost the primary. And, Jerry Brown, who won the Democratic primary, is afraid to clarify his position on taxes. The two-thirds majority to raise taxes (i.e., on the rich)—is a major problem. Although, I like his agenda of humility, living without our means—with governance based on honesty, frugality, and invocation. I am a little worried about innovations: derivatives, CDS, CDO, option ARM, and Freddie Max and Fannie Mae were innovations. If, people don't vote intelligently, we are headed for harder times.

Posted 7/29/10

MY MISTAKE

"A heavy progressive tax upon wealth of death of owner, is not only desirable, it is strictly just."—-Andrew Carnegie

I posted on 7/2/09—article entitled: The Killing of the Estate (or Inheritance) Tax and Partial Resurrection—the Obama 2010 budget passed by the House and Senate made permanent: the estate tax exemption at $3.5 million single filers: $7 million couples: at the 2009 tax rate of 45%. That is a mistake. The budget footnote reads: "The estate tax is maintained at its 2009 parameters." This misled a number of Internet news outlets, where I get my information; therefore, I was misled.

Here is a couple examples:

Barack Obama's Budget Quietly Resurrects the Death Tax for 2010....[online.WSJ .com]

FOXNews.com—Obama's Budget Resurrects 'Death Tax'

Congress passed Obama's 2010 budget—not this tax proposal in the budget, that requires separate passage. HR 4154—set the estate tax at these levels and was passed by the House: 225-200 in December of 2009--but, it was blocked by the Senate. That means: the repeal of the Estate Tax—called the "Death Tax" by opponents—for the year 2010 is still in effect.

President Obama favors the repeal of the estate repeal for the year 2010—contained in the 2001 $1.35 billion Bush tax cut. Why, this anti-democratic and irresponsible tax cut was not repealed in 2009 is disturbing: it means the plutocracy still controls the congress. HR 4154 is sponsored by Earl Pomerroy (D-ND) and none of the 11 co-sponsors are Republicans. They want the death tax repealed—permanently.

One of the main foes of the estate tax is the Policy and Taxation Group—or PATG. Their arguments are bogus:

- They claim it is one of the most despised taxes. It is by the rich and super rich who oppose it: not the majority of people.
- They claim earnings have been already subject to the income tax, Social Security tax, and other taxes—or double taxation. That is only partially true. The Poterba-Weisbenner study—found that estates worth more than $1 million were 36.4 percent untaxed capital gains—over $10 million 56.4 percent. True, they paid income taxes, but not enough and left us with a big debt. One big reason: the top income tax rate has been cut in half—since 1980. The Social Security tax is not a valid argument: this money is returned to taxpayers in the form of retirement and Medicare benefits. And other taxes, such as state, do not pay for the expenses of the federal government.
- The estate tax generates less than 2% of total federal revenues while costing the government and taxpayers approximately the same amount for enforcement and compliance. The reason it produces so little revenue: lawmakers have increased the exemption—so that, only 0.29 percent of estates are subject to the estate tax. The cost of enforcement and compliance can be solved by simplifying the tax code.
- That the estate tax is a job killer. The estate tax has nearly been phrased out: from 2001 to 2009 and the rate of unemployment increased from 5.8 to 10.2 percent. The estate tax was a low 20% from 1926 to 1932 leading up to the Great Depression. That is a scare tactic used on all tax increases (on the rich).

These are five ways plutocratic lawmakers reduced the estate tax to a small fraction of what it was—since 1976:

1. increased the estate tax exemption
2. deceased the estate tax rate
3. increased the annual gift tax exemption
4. increased the lifetime gift tax exemption
5. increased the GST exemption

There are six ways lawmakers have allowed rich-taxpayers to circumvent the estate —or death tax:

1. tax-free inter *vivos* transfers of wealth
2. irrevocable life insurance
3. family foundations
4. various kinds of trusts
5. charitable contributions
6. transfer of estate to surviving spouse

From 1942 to 1977 the top estate tax rate was 77% and the exemption: $60,000 (i.e., remained constant for 35 years). In 1976, 7.65 percent of estates were subject to the tax. This all changed in the next 33 years: from 1977 to 2010. The estate tax exemption was increased to $120,667 in 1977, to $134,000 in 1978, to $147,333 in 1979, to $161,563 in 1980, to $225,000 in 1982, to $275,000 in 1983, to $325,000 in 1984, to $400,000 in 1985, to $500,000 in 1996, to $600,000 in 1987, to $625,000 in 1998, to $650,000 in 1999, to $675,000 in 2001, to $1 million in 2002, to $1.5 million in 2004, to $2 million in 2006, to $3.5 million in 2009. The top tax rate was reduced from 77 percent to 45 percent [during the same period]. In 2009, only 0.29 percent of the estates were subject to the tax. The Bush 2001, $1.35 trillion tax cut called: *The Economic Growth and Tax Relief Reconciliation Act*—repealed the estate or "death tax" as Bush calls it—for 2010. That was based on the projection: his economic growth and tax relief plan would produce a $4.5 trillion surplus in ten years. That projection was obviously wrong: over $5.3 trillion in deficits were added to the National Debt in instead [not counting off-budget deficits). So in 2010, we have no estate (or inheritance) tax, and multi-million and billion dollar estates will be transferred to heirs tax free—and the Senate refuses to budge.

President Obama favors—repealing the Death Tax repeal for the year: 2010, but, he has not been successful in congress—so far. Republicans: representing the rich and super-rich want to eliminate the tax—permanently.

I checked the voting record of senators of the 111th congress:

35 Republicans voted: YES to repeal the estate tax: two Republicans voted NO.

34 Democrats voted: NO to repeal the estate tax: five Democrats voted YES. Senator Evan Bayh (IN)—voted: yes and no to repeal.

Two Independents: voted NO. The rest of the senators: did not vote on this bill; so, the Senate is about evenly divided.

The temporary and permanent repeal of the estate tax: would be harmful to the US—for a number of reasons. One big reason: we have a projected deficit of $1.47 trillion for 2010—and a National Debt of $13.2 trillion—and rapidly growing.

Senators Blanche Lincoln and Jon Kyl—amendment, SA 873, would increase the exemption to $5/10 million and lower the estate tax rate to 35%. That would exclude all estates—except .14 percent. That is almost total repeal.

The Sanders (I-VA)-Harking (D-IA)-Whitehouse (D-RI)-Brown (D-OH) Responsible Estate Tax Act is the best bill in congress. The tax rate above $3.5 million, but not over $10 million 45%; above $10 million, but not over $50 million 50%; over $50 million 55%, and a 10% surtax on estates valued over $500 million: $1 billion for couples.

The estate tax exemption: $3.5/7 million.

And the good thing: it is retroactive to Jan. 1, 2010—and would close some estate tax loopholes.

The worst bill in congress is sponsored by Representative Kevin Brady (R-TX). It would permanently repeal the estate tax. Warren Buffett has said, repealing the estate tax would be a terrible mistake. The repeal of the estate tax, when fully in effect, is projected by the Center on Budget and Policy Priorities to cost $808 billion over a decade. Add $222 billion for interest—the cost to borrow that money for government expenditures—in the absent of the tax.

Let's see what congress does: President Obama plans to block the estate tax from disappearing in 2010. If, he does not: that means: he has not pushed hard enough—and/or the plutocracy rules the congress: not the people.

One of the main websites that advocates keeping the estate tax—is FairEconomy.org. Check it out. They call it a fair tax, as I do in principle. Fairness depends on design. This site also refutes many of the phony arguments put forth by opponents of the estate tax—or as they call it: the "Death Tax."

I have written a book entitled: *The Estate Tax and Politics,* published in 2006. So far, I have sold only two copies. I gave 15 copies to people of interest; so far, I have received no reviews, comments, or replies.

I agree with Ray D. Madoff, a professor at Boston College Law School, who says: in an article in the Los Angeles Times 7/6/10:

"Repeal of the estate tax promotes concentrations of enormous wealth that harms our democracy."

He also refutes the double-taxation argument.

He asks the question: "Why should inherited wealth receive a free pass?" My answer: it should not. He says: "Congress (i.e., by repealing the estate tax) is giving up a valuable source of revenue." If, HR 4154—fails to pass the Senate: the government will lose about $233.6 billion over ten years. It is better than nothing—however, I believe S. 3533 is a much better bill.

He says: "Money raised from taxing inheritances could be put to good use: alleviating the tax burden for the less well off, funding programs that benefit the country as a whole or reducing the debt that we are passing on to our children."

He gives reasons: why the wealthy—have different concerns—than the general population:

...."they have privatized education for their children, privatized security for their homes, and privatized medical care through no-insurance concierge doctors." He says, out tax polices—in recent past—

have increased the gap between the rich and poor: he says, "it is not too late to change course yet again."

He says, they have acquired this tremendous wealth—by changes in the tax code—since 1976.

This is my estate and gift tax plan for debt reduction:

Twelve marginal estate tax rates from 10% to 65%: the exemption: $500,000 for single filers: $1 million for joint filers. The estate tax on family farms and businesses on the first taxable $3/6 million—operated by family heirs—would not be payable until sold—or liquidated. The estate tax is fair, because, people, the country's natural resources, and the government contributed to wealth building.

This is my Estate Tax Table for 2011:

brackets			tax rate
$0	to	$1 million	10% [after exemption]
1 million	to	2 million	15%
2 million	to	4 million	20%
4 million	to	8 million	25%
8 million	to	16 million	30%
16 million	to	32 million	35%
32 million	to	64 million	40%
64 million	to	128 million	45%
128 million	to	256 million	50%
256 million	to	512 million	55%
512 million	to	1.024 billion	60%
1.024 billion and over			65%

I would add one provision to the estate tax—regarding family farms and businesses; that is, reduce the estate tax owed on the first taxable $3/6 million—10% per year—operated by family heirs—reducing it to zero in ten years—and, if sold or liquidated: the applicable estate tax would be due.

THE NEW GIFT TAX

I would scrap the present united gift and estate tax law designed: to permit huge inter vivos transfers of wealth tax-free. I would replace it with a fair and simple design: I would make large gifts—or inter vivos transfers of wealth subject to the Gift Tax.

Here is how it would work:

The donor would report gifts exceeding $1,000 per year to the IRS—on tax returns.

The donee would report gifts exceeding $1,000 per year on his income tax returns. There would be a $5,000 per year exclusion on total taxable gifts received.

The donee would pay the gift tax.

Gifts or inter vivos transfers of wealth—larger than $10,000—would be subject to the Gift Tax Tables—payable at the time of transfer: the tax would go to the IRS: the balance to the donee.

That can be done—by setting up an account at the bank: that handles inter vivos transfers of wealth.

Certain types of gifts: non-taxable.

The gift and estate tax rates should be different, because, one is annual—the other lifetime: and the heritance tax, should be different than the gift and estate tax: This is my Gift Tax Table for 2011

brackets			tax rates
$0	to	$10,000	10% [after exemption]
10,000	to	20,000	15%
20,000	to	40,000	20%
40,000	to	80,000	25%
80,000	to	160,000	30%
160,000	to	320,000	35%
320,000	to	640,000	40%
640,000	to	1,280,000	45%
1,280,000	to	2,560,000	50%
2,560,000	to	5,120,000	55%
5,120,000 and over			60%

Professor Jeffrey Kinsler of the Elon University of Law states: "Briefly stated, the annual exclusion is the single largest loophole in the transfer tax system, and it has, in effect, converted the U.S. comprehensive estate and gift tax scheme into a system of welfare for the wealthy. If, Congress is serious about reforming U.S. welfare programs, the annual exclusion should be a key part of Such reform."

The gift tax exclusion has been rapidly increased—like the estate tax exclusion—from $3,000 in 1984 to $13,000/26,000 in 2009. In 20 years, $520,000 can be transferred to a child tree-free: $2,080,000 for 4 children: no limit on the number of persons, no limit on the number of years. Plus, there is life-time $1 million gift tax exemption. And, the donee—pays no gift tax: whether it is $10,000 or $1 million. That is not fair, when income from labor is taxed. And, there is no bill in congress that fixes that bloated gift—or *inter vivos* transfer of wealth—tax loophole.

OPTION TWO: replace the estate tax with an inheritance tax: it would look like this. The testator or person making the will—would be given a $500,000 tax exemption to be given to one person or divided among people in his/her will or testament—or inheritors. The remainder of the recipients will not receive a tax exemption. It would be limited to $500,000 per person: $1 million married couples. This is my Inheritance Tax Table for 2011.

Brackets			Tax Rate
$0	to	$100,000	10% [after exemption]
100,000	to	$200,000	15%
200,000	to	$400,000	20%
400,000	to	$800,000	25%
800,000	to	$1,600,000	30%
1,600,000	to	$3,200,000	35%
3,200,000	to	$6,400,000	40%
6,400,000	to	$12,800,000	45%
12,800,000	to	$25,600,000	50%
25,600,000	to	$51,200,000	55%
51,200,000	to	$102,400,000	60%
102,400,000 and over			65%

The heirs or recipient would pay the tax.

Family farms and businesses would be treated the same—as under the estate tax—as hitherto foresaid.

THIRD OPTION: a combination estate and inheritance tax: dividing the tax between the decedent and heirs. I would use **S 3533, The Responsible Estate Tax Act,** on large estates—and combine it with my inheritance tax table for individuals. The inheritance tax would apply on income up to the $3.5/7 million exemption. Above that level, S 3553—would be levied on estates at 50% reduced tax rates:—before distribution. Heirs or recipients of the estates assets—would pay the inheritance rate at 50% reduced tax rates. That is not double taxation: because the two halves are joined. The goal to collect back taxes owed for the last 30 years, to pay annual government expenses, correct the disproportion share of wealth held by the top 1 percent, and to bring the national debt ratio to GDP down to 40%.

FOURTH OPTION: give the people three options: estate, inheritance, or hybrid: what fits their situation best.

People must realize, if, the estate [or death} tax is repealed: paying off the national debt must come from the wages, income, and business profits of the living—rather than the dead, who created most of it.

Consider these latest statistics from the Business Insider:

- 83 percent of all U.S. stocks are in the hands of 1 percent of the people.
- 66 percent of the income growth between 2001 and 2007 went to the top 1 percent.
- In 1950, the ratio of the average executive's paycheck to the average worker's paycheck was about 30 to 1. Since the year 2000, that ratio has exploded to 300 to 500 to one.
- The top 1 percent of U.S. households own nearly twice as much of America's corporate wealth as they did just 15 years ago.
- Despite the financial crisis, the number of millionaires in the United States rose a whopping 16 percent to 7.8 million in 2009.

- Only the top 5 percent of U.S. households have earned enough additional income to match the rise in housing costs since 1975.
- The bottom 50 percent of income earners in the United States now collectively own less than 1 percent of the nation's wealth.

Plus: the after tax income of the top 1 percent increased 256% from 1979 to 2006: the bottom fifth: 11%. **Source: CBO**

Plus: the average federal tax rate of Top Income Groups: from 1970 to 2004—decreased:

- the top 0.01% from 76% to 35%
- the top 0.1% from over 60% to 35%
- the top 1% from about 48% to 35%

Source: Thomas Piketty and Emmaneul Saez

Therefore, much of the National Debt that grew from $830 billion in 1980 to $13.2 trillion by mid-2010—is back taxes owned by the rich and superrich, that had their income, capital gains, dividend—and estate and gift taxes reduced by President Reagan and George W. Bush. The Reagan and Bush tax cuts were paid for in part, by raiding the Social Security Trust Fund of $2.5 trillion and spending it off-budget—making budget deficits appear smaller than they were: add the cost of the Iraq and Afghanistan wars, which have not been paid for. They are big reasons why, a heavy progressive tax on the estates of the deceased—or an inheritance tax is not only desirable, but strictly just—to pay for the big National Debt—that the deceased left us with—and what the recipient owes for government expenses: s/he incurs.

UPDATE

Congress, late in 2010—passed HR 4853—containing a provision to increase the estate tax exemption to $5/10 million and lower the tax to 35%—beginning Jan.1, 2011. That is wrong, only 0.14 percent of estates would be affected. That is very close to total repeal. That is the goal of the Republican

Party. Obama caved in and signed the bill. This package of tax cuts is bad for the nation and should be repealed. Is it likely? No, because now, Republicans control the House. This means: the Bush tax cuts, mostly, on the wealthy—will remain in-effect for Obama's four years in office, except the estate tax was lowered more. The super-rich class won again.

And, now that the Republicans regained control of the House, they are not satisfied with reducing the estate tax to the bone—Rep. Kevin Brady (R-Tx) has introduced HR 1259—the Death Tax Repeal Permanency Act of 2011. Don't be fooled by their phony arguments. This bill is evil. Plutocrats refuse to pay part of the debt—they created during their life-time—from under taxation. That is the National Debt. There is no inheritance tax in Russia, Syria, Egypt, Saudi Arabia, Mexico, Hong Kong, India, Kuwait, Bahrain, Yemen, Jordan, United Arab Emirates, Qatar, and Libya. Once the superrich gain power, they are nearly impossible to get rid of—without civil war—or popular uprising. They control the Army and own or control the mass media and are able to misrepresent things—or omit relevant facts—and blindfold the public. Don't let that happen to the United States.

Nine reasons why the estate [or inheritance] tax is just and desirable:

1. the government needs the revenue
2. deceased owes it
3. the recipient owes it
4. to pay government FY expenses and benefits
5. to pay off the national debt.
6. to redistribute hyper-concentration of wealth
7. it prevents a plutocracy from forming....
8. repeal would be harmful....
9. it is a fair tax—if properly designed—it is not fair to dump the debts of the deceased on the next generation—or NEW BORN.

Posted 8/13/10

JUDGE VAUGHN WALKER IS WRONG!
REVISED

He says, Proposition 8—"violates the Equal Protection Clause of the 14th Amendment." No it doesn't.

This is the first half of the clause of the 14th Amendment, he is referring to: **"No State shall make or enforce any law which shall abridge the privileges or immunities of citizens of the United States."**

First of all, privileges and immunities are not the same thing: privileges give you the right to do something: immunities protect you from something—referring to the laws of the United States. Proposition 8 does not do that—i.e., violate the civil rights of the federal government; because, same sex marriage is not a right of the Bill of Rights. The California Supreme Court ruled in 2009, Proposition 8 was a legal amendment to the state constitution; so, this lawsuit does not concern, whether, Prop 8 violates California laws.

Tell me where: Proposition 8 violates the civil rights of gays and lesbians: freedom of speech, to gather in public, bear arms, right to counsel, protection from excessive bail and fines, cruel punishment—or federal laws. It does not.

The 14th Amendment—main purpose—was to grant slaves the same rights as citizens—and prevent states from abridging these rights and protections. Nothing in the 14th Amendment—makes same sex marriage a right.

The second part of this clause: **"nor shall any State deprive any person of life, liberty, or property, without due process of law, nor deny to any person within its jurisdiction the equal protection of the laws."**

Proposition 8—does none of these things.

What the judge has done—is twist the law to conform to his agenda—a practicing homosexual.

This is not the right person to judge this lawsuit—it should not be decided by no less than three judges.

In the absent of federal law: state voters can make laws—governing marriage: based on what they think is moral and their best interest. If, the US Constitution—prohibits states from defining: marriage—as between a man and woman; than, the constitution is wrong. I don't believe it does that.

California voters passed Proposition 8 by a 52.3% majority: it is legal—it cannot be overturned by a gay-activist judge; because, he thinks same sex marriage should be legalized.

He says, Proposition 8—"disadvantages gays and lesbians without any rational justification." That is his opinion; but, it is up to the voters to decide—not him.

It is not right for a single gay-activist judge—to overturn the vote of 7 million Californians—by perverting: the meaning and purpose of the 14th Amendment—to conform to his personal feelings. He can personally, favor same-sex-marriage, but, it is up to the people to decide the matter.

All powers not given to the federal government by the Constitution go automatically to the people or the states. That is the tenth right of the Bill of Rights. The California voters have spoken! Proposition 8 states: "only marriage between a man and woman is valid—or recognized in California."

Judge Walker says, the majority of California voters' support of Proposition 8 is irrelevant, as "fundamental rights may not be submitted to [a] vote." In order words, you can't vote a law into existence—that violates fundamental rights; but, Proposition 8 does not do that—because, same sex marriage is not part of the Bill of Rights—or any other federal law.

Until—the US Constitution is amended to make same-sex-marriage a right; the States have the right to pass laws based on what they think is right—and best for society governing marriage. What the federal judge is saying, banning same sex marriage by states is unconstitutional; because, there is no valid reason to so. However, in 2008, the majority of Californians feel there is. He claims their beliefs and reasons are irrational and passé.

Whether, you like it or not—all rights or privileges of the United States have been modified—or restricted. I want to remind you—the US Constitution is not a perfect—or complete document—and has been amended many times—and provides for the means to do so. The Bill of Rights were the first ten amendments.

However, in some cases, it is not clear and should not be considered: written in unbendable stone. Absolutely, no abridgements—of any right— is absurd. Proposition 8 is putting marriage in the legal terms—that has been the institution of mankind since the dawn of history. Prior to now—this definition has been considered axiomatic or self-evident. Proposition 8 has put into legal terms—what has been an institution for time immemorial. It is legal.

Judge Walker's conclusion—after hearing the evidence in his 136 page ruling or opinion—is strongly bias. He alone—has decided: what is good and bad for California and perverted the intent and meaning of the 14th Amendment to fit his agenda. Jerry Brown, the Attorney General of California, is also wrong on this issue. He agrees with Judge Walker. He says, "Proposition 8 violates the equal protection guarantee of the 14th Amendment." He misstated the meaning of the 14th Amendment by adding the word **guarantee** and leaving out the words—**of the laws [within its jurisdiction].** California's Proposition 8 does not deny gays and lesbians the equal protection of the laws within its jurisdiction. The Fourteenth Amendment—refers, primarily, to rights in the constitution. The right to marry is not included. The authority to regulate marriage is given to the States. They can make laws to serve their best interests: they can ban marriage to the same sex, marriage to people incarcerated, incestuous marriage, adults with minors, etc. Nothing in Proposition 8 denies gays and lesbians equal protection of federal laws—or the Bill of Rights. Until same-sex-marriage is a right—granted by federal law—there is no violation.

Proposition 8 does not deny gays and lesbians equal protection of the laws of California. Gays and lesbians have the right to marry the opposite sex. That is the law. The right to marry the same sex—is not a California enacted law by the legislative process. The Fourteenth Amendment—does not guarantee—no privilege or right—will be abridged—because, they all have been.

Jerry Brown has the belief—the constitution guarantees gays and lesbians the right marry [the same sex]. It does not. That right has not been enacted. Nor, is banning same-sex-marriage a violation of the constitution. It is up to the people to decide—and they have.

I wish he would read the Preamble to the Constitution—"we the people of the United States, in order to form a more perfect union"—you can disagree on what is more perfect union, but, one gay-activist judge cannot void the vote 7 million Californians. He is irrational and bias. Proposition 8 does not violate any fundamental right in the US Constitution—or Bill of Rights.

If, you look at the US Constitution, the subtitle under the 14th Amendment—is civil rights. The 14th Amendment—refers to these rights. Marriage is not included. It is the authority of States to regulate. So, how can Proposition 8—be unconstitutional. If, it is unconstitutional to make a law defining marriage—as between a man and woman; than, the constitution is wrong. This is the worldwide—institution.

Meg Whitman, the Republican candidate for governor, says: "I believe marriage should be between a man and woman." Judge Walker says, to codify those sentiments would violate the US Constitution. He is nuts.

Carly Fiorina, the Republican candidate for US senator, says: "The people of California spoke clearly on this issue at the ballot box in 2008." It does not violate federal laws; because, marriage is not part of the Bill of Rights. If, it were: the 14th Amendment would mean: you can not deny liberated slaves, or people of other races, nations and religions—the right marry. The Founding Fathers were not thinking of giving gays and lesbians the right to marry the same sex; because, these relationships were considered sinful—and in some states a crime. Today, homosexuals account for well over 50% of the AIDS cases in the United States: 2-5 percent of the population. The average homosexual has more partners per year—that the average straight in a life-time. Gays and bisexuals are the main transmitters of the Aids virus. It cost $300,000 to take care of each AIDS victim—sky rocketing medical insurance rates. Homosexuals also account for the bulk of syphilis, gonorrhea, and Hepatitis B, the "gay bowel syndrome', tuberculosis, and cytomegalovirus. Homosexual statistics are not pretty: 41% say they have had sex with strangers in public restrooms, 28% admit to 1,000 partners or more in life time. Homosexuals account for 70-80 percent of hepatitis cases in San Francisco. Let's look at all the facts.

Same-sex-marriages [or unions] were never a fundamental right—in the US or anyplace in world—until recently. The legalization of same sex marriage in Massachusetts in 2004 was by a judge—not the people. That is what is called: legislating from the bench: that violates the constitution.

The Founding Fathers thought man's inalienable or fundamental rights were endowed by their Creator. So, Judge Vaughn Walker is dead here. There is no evidence that same-sex marriage is a divine right.

Therefore, people must decide, if—same-sex marriage meets the test of this key part of the Declaration of Independence: [laws or rights that are] **the most wholesome and necessary for the public good.**

Traditional marriage fits that description.

Here is where Judge Walker made a mistake—his homosexual feelings—has clouded his ability to think straight. In his opinion, he said: Prop. 8 violates Equal Protection. It does not. Marriage is not a protection. It is a privilege or right. The Fourteenth Amendment does not use the term: equal privilege: there is a difference. Equal protection of the laws—is protection from human acts, such as: rape, assault, cruel punishment, excessive fines, punishment without trial, fraud, etc. Prop. 8 does not deny gays and lesbians equal protection of the laws. Therefore, his wording is wrong. It does abridge privilege—the right to get married to the same sex—for good reasons. The 14th Amendment does not use the term equal privilege. Marriage is a privilege or right of the law—not a protection. All privileges or rights are modified. The police have the right to carry a gun; because, it serves a useful purpose—public security—not the public, some people are on the no-fly list, felons don't have the right to keep and bear arms, the freedom of speech has restrictions, polygamy is banned, some public gatherings are declared illegal, driver licenses can be revoked, etc.

States have the right to make laws, within their jurisdiction, decide what is right and wrong—and beneficial—or harmful to its state. Judge Walker does not have the right to make that determination for Californians. He thinks there is no valid reason to deny same sex-marriage. He says, "moral disapproval" was not enough to save the voter-passed proposition 8. The problem with that—some people do.

Some people—think it does not fulfill the principal purpose of marriage. Technically, the Fourteenth Amendment—applies to civil rights—in the constitution at the time the 14th Amendment was ratified—in 1868. The Founding Fathers would—probably—want the right to modify their statement: concerning subsequent—or future enacted rights—or privileges.

For example, the 15th Amendment prohibits denial of suffrage based on race—or former Negro slaves. However, the right to vote has restrictions: the young, the insane, felons in prison, and in some states: a literacy test. Those abridgements don't violate the constitution. However, the right to marry the same sex—has never been a fundamental right under the Bill of Rights or the US Constitution.

That requires three-fourths of state legislatures to ratify—the same as the Bill of Rights, the first ten amendments.

If, same-sex-marriages are legalized—they will receive the numerous tax benefit of filing jointly and will receive other legal and tax benefits of married couples, such as: the transfer of estate to surviving spouse and double the estate tax exemption, unlimited tax free gift to spouse, Social Security [i.e., espousal survivor's benefits} and will receive the same Medicare and employer healthcare benefits as married couples. The government will receive less taxes and cost of these programs will increase. I don't believe they deserved these tax and legal benefits. Nobody is here, because of same sex marriages. This is one disadvantage.

One should look at all the legal and tax—consequences

Judge Walker has single handedly—struck down an institution going back before recorded history and recognized by all nations. He says, the exclusion of same-couples from marriage is "an artifact of time when the genders were seen as having distinct roles in society and marriage. That time has passed." Having that viewpoint—he should have recused himself from this case: he is bias. Men's and women's reproductive organs have not changed. Their roles, in this respect have not changed.

However, whether you agree or disagree: Judge Walker's ruling is wrong, because, he also misconstrued the law. Proposition 8 does not deprive gays and lesbians of life, liberty, or property, without due process. Nor does it deny them equal protection of the laws. Gays and lesbians have the protection of all the laws of California and the US Constitution. They don't have the right to marry the same sex; because, that is not a California or federal right. Therefore, his ruling is off-the-tracks.

All rights and privileges can be modified. For example, the privilege to drive a vehicle in California—has abridgements. That is not unconstitutional.

Then, why does banning same sex marriage violate the US Constitution: Judge Walker says: there is no valid reason to do so. He says, California "has no interest in differentiating between same-sex and opposite sex unions." Actually, there is a mankind survival difference: one is reproductive—and one is not. I think he should let Californians make that judgment.

Governor Schwarzenegger cheered the [perverted] ruling. As I have said before, he is a dumbbell—and this is proof. He said it "affirms the full legal protections and safeguards I believe everyone deserves." Everybody does not deserve the same privileges or rights. He does not understand English. What the judge's ruling does, it overturns—Proposition 8—passed by the majority of people—stating: only marriage between a man and woman is valid—or recognized in California—based on faulty and bias thinking.

The ruling destroys a fundamental safeguard. Schwarzenegger added: we should treat "all people" with "equal respect and dignity." I am not going to treat gays and lesbians with the same respect as mothers and fathers.

Add Major Villaraigosa to the list. He also cheered the ruling. He wrote on Twitter: "Because a judge had the courage to stand up for the constitution of the United States, prop 8 has been overturned." He will say or do anything to get the vote of gay and lesbian community. He does not understand the US Constitution—or English. The constitution does not guarantee gays and lesbians the right to marry the same sex. Nor, does Proposition 8—violate the US Constitution.

Upon hearing the ruling: Gov. Schwarzenegger and Attorney General Jerry Brown filed legal motions asking that same-sex marriage be allowed to resume immediately: I find that appalling. I believe rights of this magnitude -- should come into existence by the vote of the people—or congress—not by judicial edict.

Thirty states ban same-sex-marriage in their constitution: striking down Proposition 8 opens the door for a flood of homosexuals coming from these states to California to get married for tax, welfare, and medical benefits.

Ron Prentice of ProtectMarriage.org. says: he going to appeal the ruling to the U.S. Circuit Court of Appeals. That outcome is unknown.

The question is: will the right to marry the same sex make California better or worst: economically, socially, and politically.

To see the effects of homosexuality on a city, look at San Francisco, a haven.

To see the effects of same-sex marriage on a state—look at Massachusetts.

I seen Elena Kagan—being sworn in on TV—she said: she would perform her duties, **"so help me God."** This case might be headed to the Supreme Court. Let's see what happens. There is a price to pay for wrong thinking.

Posted: 12/9/10

TWEETS (for December)

David Stockman

Did you see and hear David Stockman, President Reagan's budget director, on 60-Minutes: Oct. 31, 2010, he says: all the Bush tax cuts should be eliminated—even those on the middle class. And he says, his own Republican Party has gone too far with its anti-tax religion.

He is absolutely correct.

He blames both parties for telling a lie with a capital B and L. But, I would add: Republicans—a little more.

Sen. Mitch McConnell (R), the senate minority leader, and Rep. John Boehner (R), the new House Speaker-elect—on issues of taxes are the people's worst enemies. They are the two big roadblocks to fair tax reform. They represent the head of the entrenched plutocracy in the Senate and House.

Mitch McConnell said on the senate floor: "I'm introducing legislation today that ensures that no one in this country will pay higher income taxes next year than they are right now."

John Boehner—called the House passed bill to end the Bush tax cuts for the richest Americans: "chicken crap."

Both are obstacles to tax reform and rated 0 by the CTJ for progressive taxation. Yes, the people-pleasing Democrats also got us into this grave financial trouble. And, that is the subject of my tweets: the debt-crisis dilemma.

The Senate

The Senate voted to block ending the Bush tax cuts for the wealthiest Americans: 56-32. That is anti-democratic: most voters oppose the GOP plan. Only 26% of Americans support extending the tax cuts for millionaires and billionaires and the Senate voted it down. It represents the wealthy, top 5 percent, who are not paying their fair share of government expenses. In my opinion, because, the Senate practices extortion and bribery to get House bills passed in the Senate, it should be abolished. It is a reincarnation of the House of Lords—that gives the small minority the power to stop tax increases on the rich—and other related House bills. They will not budge unless bribed.

David Stockman calls it an "absolute" for the Republican Party—something that can't be questioned.

This is what Sen. Bernie Sanders said, "I think for a Democratic president, a Democratic House, and a Democratic Senate to be following the Bush economic philosophy of tax breaks for millionaires and billionaires is absolutely wrong public policy and absolutely wrong politically."

He is absolutely right. The deficit for fiscal 2010: $1.42 trillion—and growing at the rate of $4.14 billion a day, $124.2 billion a month, and for 2011: $1.49 trillion: that demands resolute action now. It should have been enacted 2 years ago—to let it snowball 2 more years is insane.

Sen. Richard Durbin said, "How can we rationalize tax cuts for the wealthiest Americans when were facing this kind of deficit." The answer: we can't and must not, but the balk of Senate Republicans act as a team—they oppose, modify, and filibuster—almost everything that the House tries to enact.

I believe, it is time to abolish the Senate: that would solve a lot of gridlock, warfare between houses, duplication of work, etc.

The constitution gave the House of Representatives the power to originate all bills to raise revenues, but it needs the stamp of approval of the Senate. This bi-cameral congress does not work well. It is obsolete. It is like two drivers and two motors in the same car: one wants to go forward, one backwards—creating constant friction.

The constitution should be changed: making the congress one house—times have changed since its ratification in 1788. The qualifications for House of Representatives should be upgraded: age raised to 40, citizen for 20 years, Master's degree in political science or similar studies, or one term in a state legislature, or pass a tough test similar to the bar examination, and the length of term raised to 4 years. That would save time and money, campaigning for re-election every 2 years, and help to prevent the hijacking of the Congress by a handful of plutocrats, who can block bills by 51 members—41, if they employ the filibuster. The bi-cameral congress does not work—efficiently. It has gotten us into our present predicament: one would work better. It would also help, if, the people would be more discriminating in whom they elect. They reelected Sen. Mitch McConnell of October of 2008, for another 6 years: a stanch supporter of the Bush tax cuts, that got us into this trouble, and continues to be a vocal anti-tax demagogue in the Senate.

The Senate also voted down—ending the tax cuts on millionaires and billionaires, that is even more unconscionable. Sen. McConnell had a big simile on his face, when these tax increases failed in the Senate. Who should pay, if the government is running a big deficit: other than the rich, who benefit the most from our GDP. The two other alternatives: the poor and the middle class. The poor can't pay much. That leaves the middle class. Yes, expenses should be cut; but, the Senate voted for the war in Afghanistan and Iraq; but refused to raise taxes to pay for it. They raided the Social Security paid-in-surplus to pay for part of it and gave the rich—three big tax cuts—instead. Now, they are balking at repayment. They use the phony argument that tax increases on the rich will hurt the economy. The part-idiot Sen. McCain argued during the presidential campaign, saying to Obama, why increase taxes now—that will halt the economic recovery underway. In other words: a recession is not the time to increase taxes on the rich, nor a time of prosperity.

Republicans argue: tax increases will kill jobs. But, the three Bush tax-cuts in 2001, 2003, and 2005—did not produce the prosperity he was predicting. Instead, it created, in part, a recession and the big debt crisis that we face today. In 2001, Bush argued the four years of budget surpluses were justification for lowering taxes, mostly, on the rich. He said, they paid too much, and instead of paying down some of the near $6 trillion National Debt, he returned it. That got him elected. That was a big mistake. Well, the Clinton budget surpluses ended in 2001. And, there has been a deficit every year since—ballooning the National Debt. It seems to me, after nine years of deficits that would be justification—for raising taxes on the rich: they paid too little, mostly, the rich. But, the idiots in congress, particularly, the Republicans, don't agree: to reverse logic. David Stockman calls it: "rank demagoguery"—not based on rational thinking.

They believe: tax cuts for the rich for surpluses and deficits are both good for the country. That is irrational thinking.

The part-idiot Sen. McCain—also credits the Bush tax-cuts for the economic recovery after 2003—that is not entirely correct. David Stockman said, it was a "fake prosperity"—he is right. It was based on tax cuts, mostly on the rich, tax-breaks, government deregulation, increased house and stock prices, expanded consumer credit spending, and government deficit spending—not true economic growth. It was delusional. Bush did his best to keep that delusion alive—by misrepresenting facts. His budget deficits did not include off budget expenses. And, just before he left office—the expending big credit prosperity bubble blew up in his face.

Now, taxpayers owe nearly $14 trillion and over 8 million people have lost their jobs. It proves: cutting taxes, increasing government spending, and expecting bigger government revenues—does not work. Bush said, his tax cuts would create jobs. Today's predicament is the long-term effects of the Bush tax-cuts and economic policies. During his administration: debt grew faster than GDP. That is a failed economic philosophy. You could, also say the same about Ronald Reagan.

When Bush took office: the national debt was $5.74 trillion: today $13.8 trillion, that is a 140 percent increase; whereas, GDP grew from $9.951 trillion to $14.929: only 40 percent—and debt to GDP ratio grew from 57.6 percent in 2000 to 94.4 percent—today. He is mostly responsible for these figures; because, his 2001 and 2003 tax cuts are still in effect. We are in real economic trouble; because, these deficits will continue, unstoppable, for the foreseeable future. And, the way the congress is constituted, we can't raise taxes on the rich—because, the Republicans stand in the way—and the Democrats continue to handout freebies—further increasing the National Debt. However, some of the freebies are justified, such as: education, welfare, medical, jobless aid, etc. This is the debt-crisis dilemma.

The House

The House voted to make permanent the middle class Bush tax-cuts: 234-188. This is also wrong: considering the growing national debt. This was a proposal to make permanent the Bush tax cuts for the middle class, individuals making under $200,000 and families $250,000—but, these figures are slightly higher than middle class: real median income [individual] is about $50,550. Even, people in the middle class are not paying their fair share of taxes and nearly fifty percent of tax filers are paying no federal income tax: that is one cause of the deficits, that hast to be corrected. These lower and middle class tax cuts also apply to millionaires and billionaires, who pay reduced taxes on these same brackets. These tax cuts are designed to include members of congress. Of all people, they least deserved it. They created the budget deficits. So, here is the problem: the Senate block taxes on the rich—and the House wants to make middle class Bush tax-cuts permanent—so, that it includes them. To get out of the debt crisis: the middle class also must pay more taxes. In 2008, the top 6% to 10% paid an average tax rate of 12.6%: the top 26% to 50% paid only 7.01%. That is well below the statutory tax rates for the middle class. They have been significantly reduced by tax credits and deductions. People think taxes are too high—because, they have committed themselves to a standard of living they can't afford. That leaves no money to pay taxes. Vice President Joe Biden went on the Larry King Show and pitched the permanent extension of the middle class Bush tax-cuts: citing what people earning $50,000 and $100,000 would save. What he failed to mention: what he and members of congress—would save. These people do not need tax-cuts. He is a sly one for backing Obama's middle class tax cut two year extension. This is done not for the good of the country—but, for Obama's reelection and tax-savings for members of congress. These people need to pay more, not less taxes. So, we have two problems: the rich who don't want to pay more taxes and the middle class: they prefer to let the national debt grow—hoping for a miracle. David Stockman says: he cringes when he hears President Obama say things like this: "I believe we ought to make the tax cuts for the middle class permanent." I agree: extending the middle class tax-cuts for ten years would cost the US Treasury $3.2 trillion. In addition, Obama wants to hand out a variety of other tax breaks for the lower and middle class, without determining how he will pay for it—that will sink the nation more in debt. For 2010, as of Dec. 8th, the cost of interest on the National Debt: $5,063 per citizen and his share of the National Debt: $44,489. Not every citizen is a taxpayer: that figure goes up for taxpayers. And, here is what some people do not fully realize: Obama's tax savings are added to your federal debt and must be repaid with interest in the future. People who receive the freebies and pay no income tax are happy. People who pay for the freebies are not so happy. That is the battle going on in the congress. The question is: have the Dems gone too far? The answer: yes and no. Then, there is the hidden debt: entitlements in the pipeline—that come due in the future—that are unfunded: that comes to $516,348 for each household. Not everybody in the household is a taxpayer, so that is a tremendous burden for taxpayers. Adding to this debt seems to me—to be unwise. The prospects for future economic growth is less that it was in the past, and when, Obama's Healthcare Reform Plan kicks in—2014, the cost of government is going up. It means higher taxes—or higher federal debt. Therefore, it is better to tackle the debt crisis now—than, let it grow: dumping our debt on future generations. Because, of the high National Debt—some built-in-benefits are no longer affordable. But, another problem: Obama is willing to compromise with Republicans: that is going to lead to bigger problems down the road. He, really, lacks wisdom and has no spine. He should have ended the Bush tax cuts on the rich two years ago, raised the capital gains tax to 20 percent, made dividends taxable under income, eliminated tax havens, and enacted a stiff estate tax on large fortunes in 2010: he did none of these things—or tried. He is a weak and ineffective president, so far.

And, Vice President Joe Biden is a numskull—for urging Democrats to back Obama's compromise with Republicans. It would be better for the country—to let all Bush tax-cuts expire at the end of 2010.

There is one Republican exception: Sen. George Voinovich, he said at an Aspen Institute luncheon: "I'm voting against everything" and to make himself clear—said: "You've got to pay for it, you've got to pay for it, you've got to pay for it." The difference between him and Obama: he is 74 (seasoned) and not running for reelection: Obama is 49 (green) and running for reelection.

Obama has agreed: to extend jobless benefits 13 months costing: $56 billion, which is not paid for—and a two year extension of the Bush tax cuts on the wealthiest Americans, which will cost about: $136 billion: adding $200 billion to the National Debt: plus other concessions for the rich and super rich, such as: a reduction in the estate tax, etc. That compromise is not acceptable. It is extortion. Rep. John Conyers (D-Mich.) called it "blackmail". That is another reason: why the Senate should be abolished. The House of Representatives would provide aid to jobless without extending the Bush tax cuts to the rich and super rich.

Rep. Peter Welch (D-Vt.)—circulated a letter urging House Democrats to oppose the deal, calling it "fiscally irresponsible" and "grossly unfair." He is right. If, this compromise goes through: it is like a fat person—choosing a banana split—rather, than go on a diet—and lose weight.

I am not done: this deal includes: extending all the Bush tax-cuts for two years: adding $700 - 900 billion to the National Debt.

The Republican's block of taxes on the rich—and the people pleasing Democrats—have got us deeply in debt—and we are headed deeper in debt with Obama at the wheel, and the two houses making the laws—and no one able to stop the coming high speed train wreck—with all aboard. It is stupid: to think, by cutting taxes more, increase spending, and expect the US to solve its growing Debt-Crisis.

Posted 12/15/10

Tweet, Tweet

On Friday, the 10th, Bill Clinton appeared with Obama in the White House briefing room and endorsed his compromise with the Republicans, saying: "I don't believe there's a better deal out there." He has lost his marbles.

The best deal out there: is for Obama to veto any bill that extends the Bush tax-cuts. That is what is best for America. It is almost—a perfect tax reform plan—that does not require congressional passage. If, some Democrats and Republicans don't like it: the hell with these un-American bastards.

Posted 12/15/10

The Moment of Truth   REVISED

The report of the National Commission on fiscal responsibility and [tax] reform—has some good parts—and some bad parts. They say, their plan would bring the debt ratio to GDP down to 35% by 2035—that is bunkum. There are too many unforeseeables—to take that serious. The Congressional Budget Office, in early 2009, did not accurately predict the federal deficit for 2010—and estimated a deficit of $912 billion for 2011, it is more likely to be around $1.5 trillion.

Defect #1: The report states the present debt to GDP is 62%: I just checked the figure on the Internet: it is 94.5%. This undermines the credibility of the report, they must not be counting intra-government debt. That is dishonest. There is difference between intra-government and public; but—both are federal debt.

Defect #2: It says, the [income] statutory rates in the US are significantly higher than the average for industrialized countries: that is false. Most—or the average taxpayer in most industrialized countries pay a higher income tax, even if you include state income taxes; because, the rates are levied on lower margins, for example:

UK—top income rate: 50% over 150,000 British pounds ($246,384)
dividends taxed at 32.5%
Germany—top income rate: 45% over 250,730 EUR ($335,978)
dividends taxed at 25%

France—top income rate: 40% over 69,783 EUR ($93,509)
dividends taxed at 25.3%
China—top income rate: 45% above 100,000 Yuan ($15,620)
50% of dividends taxed at regular rates
Japan—top rate: 40% + 10% (local tax) over 18 million Yen ($216,000)
50% of dividends taxed at regular rates
South Korea—top income rate: 38.5% over 88 million Won ($77,080)
including dividends and capital gains
Netherlands—top income rate: 52% over 54,367 EUR ($72,851)
15% withholding dividend tax, 1.2% tax on total value of shares
Australia—top income tax rate: 45% over $180,000
dividends taxed as income

Compare these figures with the US top income tax rate: 35% over $379,150. Dividends top rate: 15%. State income taxes: 0 - 10.5%. But, the statutory rates are only part of the tax code. You have to include the tax deductions, tax credits, tax free incomes, etc.

For example: a family of four making $50,000 pays no federal income tax and gets a cash refund after standard and personal deductions, child tax credits, and the MWP refundable tax credit.

I would venture to say—there is no country in the world that has an income tax, where a family of four making $50,000 would pay no income tax, let alone get a refund.

The US, therefore, is one of the lowest taxed industrialized nations in the world, because of the numerous tax deductions and federal tax rates are levied on higher margins, and particularly on the wealthy, because long term capital gains (i.e., over 1 year) and dividends, two main sources of their income, are taxed at 15%. Because, incomes in the US are many times higher than other industrial nations of the world—higher marginal income tax rates are justified. For example, in 2004, the ratio of CEO pay to worker pay: US 475 to 1, UK 22 to 1, France 15 to 1, Germany 12 to 1, Japan 11 to 1, etc.

Defect #3: Reducing the income tax to three rates: 8, 13, and 23—recommended by the commission: will make the tax code more unfair. Less marginal tax rates—makes the tax code less fair. The US income tax code should have at least 15 to 30 marginal tax rates; because, of the range of income from bottom to top. According to the report, the top 23% tax rate would be levied on income over $174,401 for individuals. You mean to say, there should be no graduation in tax rates from someone earning: $200,000 and someone earning: $10 million—or $100 million. That is a grossly unfair tax code. It was designed by plutocrats—for the benefit of rich men.

The elimination of itemized deductions is good. But, that does not justify these low tax rates. The top rate should be 70 percent—on income over $10 million: based on today's National Debt-Crisis. That is not unfair. The commission said, the top rate must not exceed 29 percent: that is where Reagan put it. And, the National Debt skyrocketed from $900 billion to $14 trillion in 30 years. Nobody earns $10 million by himself: it takes a work force, natural resources exploitation, national security, an educational system, infrastructure building and repair, public transportation, public healthcare, etc. Twenty-nine percent for the nation and 71 percent for the self—over $10 million that is grossly unfair. The top rate of 29 percent will not bring the debt to GDP ratio down to 35% in 25 years: the rates are too low and congress, probably, will not implement all the cuts in government expenses—recommended by the commission. After World War II, it took a top income tax rate of 70 to 91% (dividends included), the estate top tax rate 77% and the exemption $60,000, and the corporation profit tax of 48 to 53% over $25,000—to bring the debt to GDP ratio from 120% to 33% in 1979. Besides, the potential for economic growth was greater. Now, we have more people, less natural resources, and more foreign competition.

To solve the National Debt-Crisis and fully implement a sensible and affordable National Healthcare Plan—all the income tax rates eliminated by Reagan must be restored; only, the brackets changed and all, or most of the cost cutting measures recommended by the commission implemented.

The repeal of AMT is good—if, you eliminate: tax loopholes, tax-breaks, and the deductions: it would not be necessary.

Putting dividends and capital gains under the income tax rates is correct: they are income. Why, should capital gains and dividends—

income from non-work—be taxed lower than income from labor—or family owned business and farm profits. It should not --these are unfair rich and superrich tax breaks.

I would not object to an exemption of 20% of dividend income; if placed under the income tax tables—and corporations paid a 20 percent profit tax.

A tapered exemption of long-term capital gains is fairer, than, an abrupt drop to 15 percent—after 365 days.

Reducing the mortgage interest deduction to $500,000 from $1 million is good and limit to one home. This tax deduction was too generous—and the big capital gains tax exemption resulted in people buying houses, not to live in, but for investments and tax shelters—like, Sen. McCain, who owned seven. These two tax breaks drove up the prices of houses for people who buy a house to live in. So, both of these tax breaks should be reduced.

Yes, the 15 cents gas tax to fully fund the Transportation Trust Fund is good, better than deficit financing. Americans could afford it, if they would eat less; nearly, 70 percent are overweight or obese. Like, eating too much, Americans waste too much energy: a tax would help conserve. And, it is a fair tax; because, it is imposed on the people that burn (or use) gasoline.

Defect #4: The estate or inheritance tax was omitted. That is a clear sign: this tax reform plan is the work of plutocrats. The WSJ—calls it "one of the most despised of all federal taxes (i.e., for the wealthy)." In 1976, the top rate: 70 percent, the exemption: $60,000—and 7.65 percent of estates in the event of death—paid the tax. In 2009, the top rate 45%, the exemption: $3.5 million—and only 3 out of 1,000 estates are subject to the tax—and Republicans want to lower the top rate to 35% and increase the exemption to $5 million for individuals and $10 million for couples: this is pure greed. The 2009 estate tax only collected about $15 billion. The repeal of the estate tax for the year 2010 by George W. Bush constitutes the legal theft of **$123 billion** owed in back taxes to the federal government. And, Obama and Democrats failed to correct it, when they controlled the House and Senate in 2009 and 2010.

UPDATE

This underlined part was, partially, true at time of this posting—the repeal of the estate tax in 2010—reactivated the underlying capital gains tax. The first $1.3 million is tax free: for surviving spouse $3 million. However, as I understand it, heirs can opt to pay the capital gains tax—if assets of the estate are sold—or pay the newly passed lower estate tax $5/10 million exemption and the new lower 35% tax rate that takes effect Jan. 1, 2011. However, the estate tax should have been fully resurrected, reformed, and made—retroactive until Jan.1, 2010.

*That figure is computed by multiplying the 1 out of 113—or .88495 % of the people that died in 2010 times the $14 trillion national debt.

Plutocrats are not only Republicans: they are also Democrats: three of each voted for this "starve the beast"—tax solution; so, they rich and superrich could pay no more than 23 to 29 percent on income. I believe the beast should not be overweight or obese; but, not starvation.

These types of people were sent to the guillotine in the French revolution: they now control the US tax code—and tell lies.

The 14 member commission failed to propose a heavy estate or inheritance tax to collect unpaid taxes; since, Reagan took office. He dropped the top income tax rate from 70 to 28 percent—and the national debt grew from $900 billion to $14 trillion in 30 years. Reagan and Bush have destroyed all the estate tax rates—except one—by increasing the exemption and reducing the top rate. The graduating tax rates must be restored and the exemption lowered. It was more fair—to collect unpaid taxes—from the estates of the deceased, who created the debt in their lifetime; than, to charge the new born—or future generations.

Defect #5: The commission's recommendation to lower the corporate statutory rate from 35% to 25%—as the price to pay for eliminated tax loopholes: that is a bad idea. Presently, the effective rate paid by the average major corporations is about half—the statutory rate. First, see how effective is—the elimination of tax loopholes in raising the effective rate—before lowering the statutory rate.

UPDATE

June 1, 2011, the CTJ released a report that a dozen big US companies paid an effective rate of 1.5% between 2008 and 2010. The problem is not the statutory rate—the vast number of corporations pays considerable less—and some far less—or zero. The problem is the gap between the statutory and the effective: first, eliminate the gap; then, lower the statutory rate. There is actually, no need to lower the statutory rate, because, no or few corporations pay it. Lowering the statutory rate is not warranted—unless—the actual profit tax paid by US corporations is excessive.

Critics—say the US corporate tax is the highest in the world—but, not what US corporations pay. Some big oil companies say they pay more than 35%—because, they include royalties paid to foreign countries.

Defect #6: The commission proposal to make corporate profit or income tax territorial. What that means: corporations would not pay US income tax on foreign source income. If that is the case, they will move their operations to the nation with the lowest tax. That will hurt American workers. They must pay some tax on foreign source income; because, they operate under the protective umbrella of the US Armed Forces—throughout the world. Since, they benefit from that protection, they must pay the difference or a percentage of foreign profits.

Defect #7: It did not include Reagan's former budget director, David Stockman's, one time 15% surtax on the rich to cut the National Debt in half. They owe it. The Reagan and Bush tax cuts are about a $7 trillion transfer of wealth to the top 5 percent of taxpayers: that made them super rich and ballooned the National Debt. In 1985, the top five percent of households, the wealthiest, had a net worth of $8 trillion. Today, after serial bubble, this top five percent have a net worth of $40 trillion. It is a fair tax: the next best thing: the heavy estate or inheritance tax.

The commission states: "the current income tax is fundamentally unfair, far too complex, and long overdue for reform." I agree with that part.

Posted 12/21/10

The Bastard

John McLaughlin, on his show (12/10/10), described extending the Bush tax-cuts on the richest Americans—as "not, soaking the rich." He is the voice of the plutocracy. In 2009, the top 2 percent paid 21% on income after all tax-breaks and deductions. If, the top rate was raised back to 39.6%, they would pay about 25.6 percent. That is not soaking the rich. Because of Bush's tax-cuts on income—and capital gains and dividends, two main sources of income of the rich, in 2006, the top 400 earned an average of $265 million and paid an average rate of 17.2 percent. That is under taxation. In 1944-45, during World War II, the top tax rate: 94% over $200,000 and dividends and capital gains were included—compare that to today's low rates. In South Korea, the top tax is 38.5% on income over 88 million Won ($77,084)—including income from capital gains and dividends. That is not soaking the rich: it is required for the government to provide the level of security and services it does—based on its economy. South Korea has a low debt to GDP ratio of 23.5% compared to the US—94.5%—and an unemployment rate of 4.8% compared to the US—9.8%. Raising the two top tax rates from 33% to 36% on income from $200,000 to $379,150 and from 35% to 39.6% on income above $379,150 including millionaires and billionaires is not soaking the rich. Those that are overcharged: those dying and losing their limbs in Iraq and Afghanistan and wealthy plutocrats refuse to pay for these two wars. John McLaughlin should be ashamed of himself. He has got things backwards: that is the definition of the Devil. Ending the Bush tax-cuts on the wealthiest Americans is not soaking the rich. The Reagan and Bush tax cuts have created a mountain of debt—that will bankrupt this country, if allowed to continue. The plutocracy tries to incite fear: increasing taxes on the rich—will kill jobs. That is a big lie: our present unemployment predicament is caused by other factors, such as: the trade imbalance, high government debt, the loss of our manufacturing base, our involvement in two costly wars, and the concentration of wealth in the hands of few: the top 1 percent own more financial wealth than the bottom 90 percent. Extending the Bush tax-cuts on the wealthy—will not solve any of these problems: it will add to the National Debt and have little effect on job-creation. Obama missed an opportunity of a lifetime, to get rid of all the Bush tax-cuts, without congressional action—by letting them expire in 2010. Instead, he made a pact with Senate Republicans (i.e., the Devil)—and extended all the Bush tax-cuts, including the wealthy, and reduced the estate tax to near extinction. This is a Big Mistake—Sell Out.

Posted: 12/22/10

The Fox and the Sloth (revised 12/27/10)

On 60 Minutes, 12/5/10, Scott Pelley said to Ben Bernanke, Chairman of the Federal Reserve, "The gap between the rich and poor in this country has never been greater, in fact, we have the biggest income disparity gap of any industrialized country in the world." And, he asked: "And I wonder where you think that is taking America?" Ben Bernanke answered: "Well, it's a very bad development" and he blamed it on educational differences. That is a dishonest answer—a small factor. The difference in income between high school and college graduates in 2008 was about 60 percent or $31,000. That does not account for the fact, the average CEO pay to average worker pay, in 2008, was 310 times greater. They can be overpaid and it's legal. And, Scott Pelley, let this bogus explanation pass without a question. The truth of the matter, the compensation of executives have skyrocketed from 1980 to the present and congress has not adjusted the minimum wage—to keep up with inflation. The top 1 percent captured half of overall economic growth from 1993—2007. From 1997—2007, during this same period, there was no change in the minimum wage. The second reason: the top 1 percent own about 50% of investment assets. And, the third big reason: the Reagan and Bush tax cuts. They reduced the top income tax rate from 70% over $108,300 to 35% over $379,000, increased the estate tax exemption from $175,000 to $3.5 million and Bush lowered the tax on capital gains and dividends to 15%, two big sources of income of the wealthy. These are the big reasons for the gap in income and wealth. Ben Bernanke did not tell the truth. He said, "it is based very much, I think, on educational differences. It's creating two societies." And, he cited: the 10% or more unemployment rate for high school graduates—compared to the 5% for college. And, he said: "It's a very big difference." There is a difference, but not a big difference. Recently, PayScale.com released a report: Colleges that bring the Highest Paycheck: this is the top figure for mid-career median salary: $136,000. Nobody is complaining about that. That is not the two societies we are talking about. We are talking about extreme rich and poor. For example, the average pay of the S&P 500 chiefs for 2009 took home: $9.27 million. And a big chunk in stock options and awards, so, that when stock prices recovery, they will pay 15% on capital gains. The annual federal minimum wage: $15,680.

It gets worst: the average compensation of among the 50 CEOs that laid off the most people: $12 million in 2009: total number laid off by these companies: 531,363. The highest paid of those CEOs: $49,653,063: number that company laid off: 16,000.

It gets worst: the highest paid CEO in 2009: $188 million. That is 11,989 times minimum wage. The top is allowed to go sky-high and the bottom kept legally low. In 1978, CEO's pay to minimum wage: 78 times: in 2005: 821 times. In addition to this: their income taxes cut in half: by Reagan and Bush, two Republican presidents. This is the growing gap between the rich and poor we are taking about. Scott Pelley is either an idiot—or highly paid by CBS—not to challenge these—phony answers—or dip deeper.

For example, he failed to ask these questions: the salaries of executives of banks that received TARP bailout money—were supposed to be restricted to $500,000; however, in 2009, the CEO of Bank of America, Citigroup, Goldman Sachs, and JP Morgan and Chase—all got big stock awards: from $9 million to $27 million. Scott Pelley failed to ask Bernanke: Is this a circumvention of the law? Do these multi-million stock awards have anything to do with the gap between the rich and poor? Is this a good or bad development—creating two societies: the rich bankers and the millions of people losing their homes to foreclosure?

If, Bernanke knew these questions were coming, or had to face a real critic: there would be no TV interview. That is a big problem. The plutocracy owns the Mass Media—and controls the news.

When he was asked what he would do to make the economy grow, he said: "cleaning up the tax code"...."closing loopholes" and "lowering rates." That is the answer of a plutocrat: the Debt-Crisis cannot be solved, unless taxes are raised, particularly on the wealthy—closing loopholes, and cleaning up the tax code.

Obama had an opportunity—to fix the problem—get rid of the Bush tax cuts—and blew it. He took the path of least resistance and kicked the Debt Crisis can down the road. That strategy will make matters worst. He is following the Bush-Bernanke-Republican Party tax-economic policy.

That policy; basically, is cutting taxes to grow the economy and create jobs. Those were the reasons given for the Bush 2001 and 2003 tax cuts; instead, the expansion of the individual and federal Credit Bubble—Broke—and created a recession, the loss of more that 8 million jobs, and added $8 trillion to the National Debt in ten years. It is based on wishful thinking—not facts.

And, Ben Bernanke defended the Bush tax cuts, saying: "We don't want to take action this year": he needs more convincing. He is an idiot.

Ben Bernanke's answer for the gap; basically, is eluding the truth (i.e., lying); because, the truth embarrasses the plutocracy, for which he works for.

It is no different in principle; than, agreeing with Hitler (evil): to get and keep a high ranking job

If, he would have criticized Bush's tax cuts, he would have never been appointed chairman of Bush's Council of Economic Advisers in 2005 and head of the Federal Reserve in 2006.

UPDATE

*Recently, I got a copy of "**Winner-Take-All Politics...**"by Jacob S. Hacker & Paul Pierson, which explains:*
Why Education Gaps Can't Explain American Top-Heavy Inequality.
Bernanke, Chairman of the Federal Reserve, should read it!

The grilling of top government officials—should be done by experts—with no questions barred—and no right to hide behind closed doors, the Federal Reserve Headquarters in Washington DC, instead of a soft-friendly rigged TV interview—like seen on 60 Minutes.

Posted 12/28/10

The Little Liar

During the week from Nov. 29 to Dec. 3—Katie Curic devoted part of the Evening News to the Deficit Crisis Dilemma—and she asked John Dickerson, chief political correspondent and analyst of State Magazine, about the debt and the Reagan tax cuts, he said: Reagan raised taxes more than he cut. That is a lie. And Katie Curic being inept, did not know the difference. That is also a problem: addressing questions to people, who defend the plutocracy—rather than criticize—and by people, who are stupid—or paid to be stupid—like, Scott Pelley and Katie Curic.

Mr. Hell No

Lesley Stahl said on 60 Minutes...."the public saw something they probably never expected from Mr. Hell No, it was called "the sob heard around the world." She was referring to Rep. John Boehner (R-Ohio), the new sworn-in House Speaker. He was dubbed Mr. Hello No—by Obama for his opposition to his legislation.

Stahl asked him, why he was so sad on election night? He told a crowd, after his victory, that he spent his whole life chasing the American Dream—and when he mentioned: he put himself through college working every rotten job there was: he choked up—and begin to sob.

Stahl was fooled by this man, when he began crying during the interview and she extended her hand and said, "I want to hold your hand"—not knowing he is equivalent to Jack, the Ripper (i.e., in congress).

Is Boehner a good congressman? Hell no. Let me enumerate the ways. Middleclass.org says: "Boehner is out of touch." Here are some of his bad votes:

No—on Restore Pay-as-You-Go Tax Amendment of 2004
No—on raising the minimum wage to $7.25 (2007)
No—on Clean Energy Act of 2007
No—on regulating the subprime mortgage industry (2007)
No—on letting shareholders vote on executive compensation (2009)
No—on Wall Street Accountability and Consumer Protection Act

No—on Affordable Health Care for American Act of 2009

No—on Jobs for Main Street Act of 2009

No—on Pay for Performance Act of 2009 (executive compensation)

No—on Credit Cardholders Bill of Rights Act of 2009

No—on Helping Families Save Their Homes Act 2009

No—on Unemployment Compensation Extension Act of 2010

No—on Legislation making major changes to the National Health Care System including Health Coverage for uninsured Americans. He is covered by the Federal Employees Health Benefit Program (FEHBP).

His net worth: $2.1 million to $7.7 million, salary for 2009: $193,000—and does not make his tax returns public. This is important: the tax returns of millionaires and billionaires should be studied—to find out how they reduce and evade taxes; if, you want to change the tax code. For example, the McCourts, owners of the Los Angeles Dodgers, had an income of $108 million from 2004 to 2010 and paid no state or federal income tax: the way we knew: it came out in the divorce.

Boehner got out of the Navy eight weeks after enlistment with a bad back during the Vietnam War. I don't buy it, without seeing the proof. He passed the physical to get in. What was wrong with his back? Did he have an injury verified by x-ray or was it an invisible back pain? We don't know. He has no problem playing golf.

Evil could be hiding in Boehner's tax returns and his Navy medical records. When, you don't make them public, there is reason for suspicion. I would like to see both, but I have no right.

Voters should demand—candidates make these things public—before—voting these shady characters into office.

Putting that aside, he said: the surtax to pay for the Afghanistan and Iraq wars was "Raiding every taxpayer's wallet for the purpose of playing politics with our national security, amounts to one of the most irresponsible proposals I've seen in a long, long time."

This statement is proof he is irrational.

He voted Yes on authorizing force in Iraq (2002).

The cost of the Iraq War to date: $748 billion.

The cost of the Afghanistan War: $380 billion, so far.

An article in the Washington Post states: this is first time in American history that—the government cut taxes as it went to war—and during war. Boehner voted to make the Bush tax cuts permanent (2002).

He voted Yes on retaining the reduced taxes on capital gains and dividends in Dec. 2005—until 2011. This was a particularly an irresponsible tax cut, because the Iraq and Afghanistan wars were in progress.

He supports the wars: he just doesn't like paying for them. Rep. Dave Obey said, the surtax is a way for "this generation" to pay for the Iraq war. I agree—that is correct. Boehner is wrong.

The citizen counterpart: to men fighting and dying on the battlefield: paying a tax to support the war: he failed in both.

He enlisted in the Navy—and got out with pain in his back—and opposes the war surtax, because it hurts his pocket book.

Is he a good American? Hell no: his refusal to support or pay the war surtax is tantamount to taxpayer desertion.

Rep. Boehner said, "Washington does not have a revenue problem. Washington has spending problem." That is false.

The National Debt; mostly, was created by the Reagan and Bush tax cuts—not supplying enough revenue to operate the federal government. He voted Yes on the $958 billion Bush tax cuts over 10 years and voted to make the Bush tax cuts permanent in 2002—and holds the same views today.

The Afghanistan war is in its tenth year and the Iraq war in its eighth year and no tax increase has been made to pay for them: that is a revenue problem. Putting the cost on America's credit card is the same as paying for it.

Boehner has signed a pledge not to raise taxes: that is tantamount to refusing to pay for the cost of two wars: he voted for. When, you authorize a war, where men die and lose their limbs and you fail to support or pay the war surtax: you are a citizen and taxpayer deserter—deserving of fine, prison or death.

The Bush administration: estimated the cost of the war: $50 - $60 billion; obviously, that was wrong. The true cost of the Iraq war: $3 trillion and beyond. Obviously, the $1.35 trillion 2001 tax cuts, the $350 billion 2003 tax cuts, and the $70 billion 2005 tax cuts were irresponsible.

To make up the difference for the loss of revenue from the Bush tax cuts, mostly, on the wealthy, the paid-in Social Security surplus was raided. Boehner voted No on strengthening the Social Security Lockbox (1999). Now, the federal government owes the Trust Fund $2.5 trillion.

2010 was the first year, more money was paid out—that was paid in—and there is no money in the Trust Fund to make up the difference; therefore, the government must raise taxes to make good the IOUs.

Boehner's pledge not to raise taxes is tantamount to refusing to pay off this debt: that constitutes misappropriation (stealing). It is like taking money from your mother's bank account—she is saving for retirement— and spending it on things you want: a new car, rent, etc.—and refusing to make good on repayment.

Boehner voted for or supported all Bush tax cuts, skewed in favor of the wealthy, like himself—and that has created a revenue problem; since, 2001, $8 trillion has been added to the national debt.

To make up this short fall: the Social Security Trust Fund paid-in-surplus was raided every year—and Boehner refuses to repay it. His solution (i.e,, increase the retirement age to 70).

He stood-by eight years without a murmur and enjoyed the Bush tax cuts on his income, while Bush raided the Social Security Trust Fund to pay for the Iraq and Afghanistan wars—and he made it easy for him to do so, by voting not to strengthen the Social Security Lockbox.

Now, he has signed the Taxpayer Protection Pledge, which amounts to a refusal to raise taxes to reimburse the Social Security Trust Fund. It is impossible to pay for the Social Security benefits coming due, that have already been paid for, without a tax increase, unless you borrow the money, which adds to the deficit. The pledge constitutes refusal to honor a debt (stealing).

He, recently, voted for a 2 year extension of all the Bush tax cuts, including those on the wealthiest Americans; despite the fact, the projected deficit exceeds more than $1 trillion for 2011 and 2012. Individuals and couples with income over $200,000 and $250,000 are not suffering from the recession. This tax cut is blatantly wrong.

Yale law school professor, Daniel Markovits said, "Extending the tax cuts for the very wealthiest Americans is frankly unconscionable." He is backed by two other Yale and Cornell university professors: Robert Hockett and Jacob Hacker—co-author with Paul Pierson, professor of political science at Berkeley, of "Winner Take All Politics: How Washington Made the Rich Richer—and Turned its back on the Middle Class."

Stahl asked Boehner, "Was it worth what you got? [referring to the $900 billion tax deal—extending the Bush tax-cuts two years]. He said, "I think its worth it. I think it will create jobs and help our economy." That is the continuation of the Bush stratagem (lie) that has failed. There is something spurious about one, who advocates the means of creating jobs—cutting his income tax. The former speaker of the House, Nancy Pelosi, said six months ago: "I believe the high-end tax cuts did not create jobs, increased the deficit, and should be repealed." She is correct.

David Stockman, Reagan's former Budget Director, said: the Bush tax cuts are "unaffordable" and extending them would be a "travesty".

The Treasury Department estimates: it will add $3.7 trillion to the National Debt in ten years—or thereabouts.

Even, Timothy Geithner, Secretary of the Treasury, said on Fox News, 9 Oct 2010: upper-class cuts bad policy. I said that back in 2003.

Despite these facts and opinions, Rep. Boehner stated after the 2 year extension: he now plans to make the Bush tax cuts permanent. He is the new pitch man for the Republican Party in the House.

Boehner told Stahl, "There're some—some things that are—very difficult to talk about—family, kids. I can't go to schools any more. I used to go to a lot of schools. And you see all these little kids running around. Can't talk about it."

And Stahl asked why?

Boehner said, "Making sure that these kids have a shot at the American dream, like I did. It's important." As he said this: he choked up and begins sobbing again during his TV interview—and this is when Stahl extended her hand and said, "I want to hold your hand." She sees him as a man with a soft-caring heart—that needed comforting. I see it differently, as a man with a guilty conscience—for destroying the American dream for kids—by piling on them this humongous national debt—and for these reasons:

He voted against the Children's Health Insurance Program Reauthorization Act of 2007 and 2008 (revised).

He voted against adding 2 to 4 million children to SCHIP eligibility

He voted against the Healthy, Hunger-free Kids Act.

These are more likely to be the reasons: why he can't face them. He is dead-beat, guilt-ridden, rich congressman. He signed a no tax increase pledge: meaning he refuses to raise taxes to pay-off the National Debt.

The income tax rates—today—are the lowest since the Great Depression, except, when Reagan lowered the top rate to 28 percent. It is not as much as a spending problem—as a revenue problem. We are suffering from high debt, because of under taxation for the last 30 years, particularly, the last ten.

And, Boehner voted to repeal the estate tax, which allows the deceased and his descendants, to escape paying for the $8 trillion debt created since, Bush took office. Anybody that votes to repeal the estate [inheritance] tax—votes for an America ruled by the rich.

Warren Buffett said, "without it, we will have an aristocracy of wealth." Ralph Nader said, "Democracy, or avaricious plutocracy." That happened when George W. Bush was in office. He cut incomes taxes, mostly, on the rich, tried to eliminate the dividend tax, lowered the tax on dividends and capital gains, lowered the estate tax and repealed it for one year (2010)— and repeatedly tried to repeal it—permanently. .

Alexis de Toqueville, a French political thinker and historian, stated: "It was the estate tax that made equality take its last step."

Rosie Hunter, a researcher, and Chuck Collins, a program director, at United for a Fair Economy wrote in article entitled: **"Death Tax" Deception:** "Abolishing the estate tax would further concentrate the nation's wealth in the hands of the super-rich at a time when the distribution of wealth is already more unequal than at any point since the 1920s."

Boehner disagrees, he voted to eliminate the estate [death] tax—April 2001. This is the goal of the Republican Party.

He also voted for raising the estate tax exemption to $5 million from $1 million (Mar. 2008), so when he dies, his children will not get stuck with paying any of the debts, he created during his life time, for example: the cost of the two wars and the siphoning off of the Social Security Security paid-in-surplus—that went into his pockets as Bush tax cuts on income.

And he calls: the pact to extend Bush tax cuts on the top 2-3 percent of the Wealthiest Americans—as the price for extending the tax cuts on the middle class: not hostage taking. He calls Obama's statement political "rhetoric". Of course, it is extortion.

Jacob S. Hacker, Yale University professor, says: "On Capital Hill, Senate Republicans are threatening to filibuster every bill until the Democrats agree to extend the Bush-era-tax cuts to all income groups."

The sticking point: the top 2-3 percent.

Rep. Jay Inslee also said, "John Boehner is holding us hostage." The extension of the middle class Bush tax cuts were agreed upon—only when, the Democrats agreed to extend the Bush tax cuts on the wealthiest Americans.

In 2006, Republicans refused to raise the minimum wage unless it was linked to a cut in the estate tax. Boehner said: "This is the best that we've got; we're going to take it."

Fortunately, Senate Democrats said No.

Boehner told Stahl, "I made it clear—I am not going to compromise on my principles. She should have asked: What are your tax principles? I can tell you: they are the principles of the Republican Party. He voted with most Republicans 97% of the times. Republicans intend to retain the Bush tax cuts, mostly on rich, come Hell or high water. Boehner was elected House Speaker to achieve that goal.

Boehner continued, "Nor am I going to compromise the will of the American people." He did—the majority of people are in favor of letting the Bush tax cuts on the wealthy—expire.

He may have realized the American dream; but, he has killed it for millions of others. These five votes mark him as a plutocrat:

(1) He voted No—on the Financial Reform Bill—aimed at correcting the defects in the financial system that led to the 2008 economic crisis. He called it a "bad bill."—"This is killing an ant with a nuclear weapon."

These statements are proof—he is insane—or the $3.4 million he received from the financial industry—affected his mind.

(2) He co-sponsored, voted Yes, and led the charge to eliminate the death [estate] tax. He believes in an America ruled by the rich. He believes he should be able to transfer his entire estate to his descendents, without the government collecting back taxes, he owes, the federal debt, he created during his life-time.

Even, if you disagree with government spending—that does not exempt you from paying the debt. That is absolute—unless you are unable: that is not the case with John Boehner, he is a millionaire.

(3) He voted No—on ending the Bush tax cuts on the wealthy, even though, the projected deficit for 2011 is well over $1 trillion.

(4) He voted—for the bill extending all the Bush tax cuts for 2 years and a reduction in the estate tax—adding $900 billion to the National Debt.

In an article in the Los Angeles Times: **And the rich get richer**—Tim Rutten wrote: "Of the several objectionable provisions in the tax compromise that congressional Republicans extorted from the Obama administration, none is more noxious than the one that all but guts the estate tax.

" Even the needless and unfair continuation of the tax reductions for families making more than a quarter of a million dollars a year merely extends a benefit already enjoyed by affluent households. Estate tax cuts, by contrast, create a whole new windfall for those who already enjoy privileges and security undreamed of by the vast majority of Americans."

(5) He voted No—on increasing the tax rate for people earning over $1 million (2008).

Boehner is a member of the Congressional Flat Tax Caucus: he does not believe—in the principle of progressive taxation.

Unfortunately, the majority of the people do.

Two-thirds of Americans favor taxing the rich to reduce the deficit—according to a Bloomberg Poll (2009).

But, Boehner has signed a pledge—not to raise taxes—even on the wealthiest Americans: meaning: he is willing to let this behemoth National Debt remain on the books—and interest paid to investors: public and foreign—for ever.

He wants to cut government costs—to reduce the debt: that is only part of the solution. The National Debt is mainly caused by the butchering of the individual and corporate tax code—by **R** & D lawmakers.

The problem with Boehner, he does not know where the middle is. The Internal Revenue Service data for 2007—shows: households with incomes above $200,000 received 47% of the taxable interest income, 60% of the dividends, and a staggering 84% of the net capital gains. That is the top 3-4 percent. Extending the Bush tax cuts on income, dividends, and capital gains, when we are facing a $1 trillion plus deficit next year—is unconscionable (i.e., the Devil).

The problem with Boehner: he does not believe in the graduating income tax.

President Franklin D. Roosevelt said in a speech to Congress in 1935: "With the enactment of the Income Tax Law of 1913, the Federal Government began to apply effectively the widely accepted principle that taxes should be levied in proportion to ability to pay and in proportion to benefits received. Income was wisely chosen as the measure of benefits and of ability to pay. This was, and still is, a wholesome guide for national policy. It should be retained as the governing principle of Federal taxation."

Boehner—does not think so.

The problem with Boehner: he [also] does not believe in the estate [inheritance] tax: two principles this country is founded on.

Theodore Roosevelt said in 1910: "I believe in a graduated income tax on big fortunes, and...a graduated inheritance tax on big fortunes, properly safeguarded against evasion, and increasingly rapidly in amount with the size of estates."

Both were put into law by President Woodrow Wilson, who regarded himself as the personal representative of the people—and the only President to hold a Dr's degree.

William Gates Sr. testified before the Senate Finance Committee that without an estate tax there will be "an aristocracy of wealth that has nothing to do with merit."

President Franklin D. Roosevelt [also] said to Congress in 1935: "I My first proposal, in line with this broad policy, has to do with inheritances and gifts. The transmission from generation to generation of vast fortunes by will, inheritance, or gift is not consistent with the ideals and sentiments of the American people."

Meizhu Lui, Executive Director of United for a Fair Economy said, "gutting the estate tax would contribute to the creation of a financial aristocracy, a permanent class based on inherited wealth. Don't the 'conservatives' understand that goes against the intentions of the Founding Fathers."

Boehner voted to repeal it 2001 and led the opposition to reinstate it in 2010—signing the Death Tax Repeal Pledge.

He is a disgusting—idiot, who reasons falsely—his loyalty is to the Republican Party—not to the American people. And, that is why: he was elected speaker of the House. They can count on him to say, Hell no—to any bill that raises taxes, particularly, on the rich: no matter how just: to reduce the staggering National Debt: Hell no, for healthcare: Hell no, for jobless aid: Hell no, for hungry kids: Hell no, to pay for the two wars: Hell no, etc.

If, Rep. Boehner was living during the French Revolution, he, probably, would have been executed with Robespierre.

Posted 2/2/11

Egypt in Crisis [revised 2/4/11]

The uprising in Egypt—basically, is caused by the widening gap between the rich and poor: 5% of the population rich, 15% middle class [and dwindling] and 80% poor. President Hosni Mubarak's family wealth estimated at $40 billion; that is an increase of more than $1 billion per year, during his 30 year reign. Much of his wealth deposited in Swiss bank accounts and invested in real estate in London, New York, and Los Angeles.

His two sons—also are billionaires.

Egypt is a plutocracy—or dictatorship of the rich—who owns or controls the Mass media; one, civil engineer said: the only people who wanted Mr. Mubarak to stay in power were rich people "afraid for their money." I am quoting from an Article in the New York Times: **Protests in Egypt Expose Rift between Rich and poor:** "These big guys are stealing all the money" said a textile worker.

The article by David D. Kirkpatrick and Mona El-Naggar states: "The widening chasm between rich and poor in Cairo has been one of the conspicuous aspects of city life over the last decade – and especially the last five."

That is quite similar to the US—and Mubarak to Bush—there has been an economic boom for some; since 1990, there has been a sharp increase in GDP, particularly in the last five years. Rich Egyptians have fled the city. They have flocked to gated communities full of big American-style homes around country clubs, etc.

One man says; "They are building housing, but not for us – for those people up high."

Whereas, 17 to 20 million Egyptians live in shantytowns or slums; typically, made of sheet metal or wood, one room with inadequate sewerage, perhaps sharing a bathroom with two or three families. One in five Egyptians live on $2 a day or less.

One reason for increasing number of poor: its population growth rate of 2.03 [2009] is too high for its level of economic development. Its population grew from less that 30 million in 1960 to over 78 million in 2010. Its GDP was lagging from 1960 to 1990, then increased, and spiked up sharply in the last five years.

Second: reason: income inequality: Quoting—the Future of Capitalism.com—it says, "Egypt's top quintile of earners has increased its share of income since 1990, while the country's bottom quintile has seen its share of the pie get smaller.

The third big reason for the growing gap between the rich and poor: taxes.

1. The top income rate is 20%—on income over 40,000 EGP—[about $6,802]. It has four rates: from 5% to 20% and stops: there is no higher graduating tax rates on higher incomes.
2. There is no tax on dividends—the income of the rich is not taxed—but income from labor is taxed.
3. There is no tax on capital gains—another source of income of the rich.
4. There is no estate or inheritance tax: most of the income of the nation flows into the hands of the rich—not taxed and under taxed—and they keep it: invest it and the rich get superrich: Egypt has 13 billionaires—all businessmen.

Wealth concentrated in the hands of a few, results in a dictatorship of the wealthy—they pay for a strong police force to enforce their laws and protect their wealth—and neglect the educational, health, and economic needs of the poor, until resentment grows and erupts into a popular uprising. That is what has happened in Egypt.

FOR LATER POSTINGS:
See my blog: www.thetaxguardian.com.